IS THERE A PUBLIC FOR
PUBLIC SCHOOLS?

IS THERE A PUBLIC FOR PUBLIC SCHOOLS?

David Mathews

Kettering Foundation Press

Dayton, Ohio

© 1996 by the Charles F. Kettering Foundation

For information about permission to reproduce selections from
this book, write to:

        Permissions
        Kettering Foundation Press
        200 Commons Road
        Dayton, Ohio 45459

This book is printed on acid-free paper
First edition, 1996
Manufactured in the United States of America
Library of Congress Cataloging-in-Publication Data

Mathews, Forrest David, 1935-
    Is There a Public for Public Schools?
    p. cm.
    Includes bibliographical reference and index
    ISBN 0-923993-02-9

Library of Congress Catalog Card Number: 96-76709
                                           CIP

C O N T E N T S

After looking inside the public schools in a series of studies that culminated in John Goodlad's *A Place Called School* (1984), the Kettering Foundation became increasingly aware of the powerful influence on these institutions of forces outside their walls. Former Governor of Mississippi William Winter, a Kettering trustee, reported that the political will for the kind of reform initiative he had led in the early 1980s had begun to wane. And the late Lawrence Cremin, another trustee and a leading American historian of education, suggested that the foundation investigate what was happening to the social and political purposes that had driven the nineteenth-century commitment to public education.

Following these leads, we undertook a series of research projects on the public and its relationship to public education, eventually accumulating a sizable body of relevant work. Though we were initially reluctant to believe what we were finding, study after study — done by different researchers using different methods and investigating different sections of the country — led us to conclude that the public and the public schools were, in fact, moving apart, that the historic compact between them was in danger of dissolving.

The foundation is indebted to everyone who contributed to the effort, especially those who helped bring the findings together in this book.

To Judy Suratt, editor-in-chief, who insisted on just the right word; to diligent research assistants David Moore, Kristin Cruset, Dana Boswell, and James Norment; to Kathy Whyde Jesse, a versatile writer and researcher who lives the issues in this book; to program officers Estus Smith, Gina Paget, and David Smith, who lent a guiding hand; to Angel George, who turned the words into type — the warmest thanks for a most productive collaboration.

To The Harwood Group, John Doble Research Associates, Public Agenda, and the others who carried out the bulk of the research, all credit for the substance of this report.

To the hundreds of citizens who brought their experiences and perspectives to the research, the greatest appreciation for sharing their deepest concerns and aspirations.

To the present trustees; to the other staff members and associates of the Kettering Foundation (where everyone's fingerprints are on everything that is produced), especially Ed Arnone and his crew, who got the manuscript into print in no time — a willing accounting of my debt to all of them.

CHAPTER 1

PUBLIC SCHOOLS—OUR SCHOOLS

Is America committed to its public schools? Of course it is. That is what I've always believed and thought that everyone else did, too. If you ask Americans about their support for public schools, they usually say, "Yes, we need them" or "It's important that we have schools that are open to everyone." Public schools educate most of America's young people — some forty million of them. Kettering research suggests, however, that this commitment may not be as unequivocal as it first appears.

Some communities are blessed with good public schools. Some observers even argue that our public schools, overall, are doing a good job.[1] Yet the experience of most Americans tells them that the nation's school system is in trouble and that the problems are getting worse.[2] Our first reaction is to

---

[1] Gerald W. Bracey, "The Fifth Bracey Report on the Condition of Public Education," *Phi Delta Kappan* 77 (October 1995): 149–160 and "Stedman's Myths Miss the Mark," *Educational Leadership* 52 (March 1995): 75–80.

[2] The Harwood Group, *How Citizens View Education: Their Public Concerns and Private Actions* ([Dayton, Ohio]: Kettering Foundation, 1993).

blame teachers and administrators for a lack of discipline and a falling-off of standards. Our second is to recognize that schools are overwhelmed by social problems not of their making. We see the causes beginning in the decline of the family and extending to a breakdown of the norms of responsible behavior. What appears to be a web of interconnected problems prompts us to say that everyone has to rally round and pull together as a community in order to combat these threats.

But that isn't happening with the public schools — we aren't rallying round them. Instead of moving closer to these institutions, Americans are moving away. People without children sometimes deny any responsibility for the schools, saying that falls on parents. Parents, however, may feel accountable for their own children but not for children generally.

Unhappily, many Americans no longer believe the public schools are *their* schools, and yet this isn't a major issue today. On the contrary, all kinds of school reorganization go on with little regard for the effect on the relationship between the public and its schools. However reasonable in their own right, market-based reforms, court decrees, increased financial control by state governments, and professionally set standards may be putting citizens at an even greater distance from the public schools. That is the most alarming implication of more than ten years of research commissioned by the Kettering Foundation on the relationship between the public and its schools. Despite a long tradition of support for public education, Americans today seem to be halfway out the schoolhouse door.[3]

Even though 50 to 70 percent of Americans indicate support for their local public schools (perhaps because people have a better relationship with institutions that are close enough to affect), this statistic may tell only half the story, masking an erosion of the historic commitment to the idea of schools for the benefit of the entire community.[4] People also like their local representatives in Congress better than they do Congress in general. But

---

3 The Harwood Group, *Halfway Out the Door: Citizens Talk about Their Mandate for Public Schools* ([Dayton, Ohio]: Kettering Foundation, 1995).

4 Stanley M. Elam, Lowell C. Rose, and Alec M. Gallup, "The 26th Annual Phi Delta Kappa/Gallup Poll of the Public's Attitudes toward the Public Schools," *Phi Delta Kappan* 76 (September 1994): 41–56.

erosion of confidence in Congress, indeed in our entire system of representative government, is both real and dangerous. By the same token, erosion of our commitment to a system of public schools should be taken very seriously. We need to listen to those who are saying that, while they would like to stand by the public schools, they can't.

My guess is that a breakdown of the contract between the public and the public schools may be one reason for the more obvious problems — dissatisfaction with the performance of the schools, difficulties in communication between administrators and the public, and lack of citizen participation. While these are all serious, a deterioration of the commitment to public education would call for more than improving test scores, doing a better job of communicating, or what is usually implied by "engaging the public."

Why doesn't "engaging the public" go far enough? Because there may be no public waiting to be engaged. That is, there may be so few people supportive of the idea of public schools — so small a community for these inherently community institutions — that school reform may need to be recast as community building. In other words, certain things may have to happen in our communities before we can see the improvements we want in our schools.

Why isn't there a public for public schools today? Our research found what other studies have reported: while Americans believe the country needs public schools, they are torn between a sense of duty to support these schools and a responsibility to do what is best for children. They are ambivalent and agonize over the dilemma. And, however reluctantly, many are deciding that public schools aren't best for their children or anyone else's.

Part of their conclusion grows out of a perception that schools are so plagued by disorder that children can't learn. Although media hype and hearsay are often blamed for this perception, the people we talked to based their conclusions on personal experience or the experience of family members and close friends. Citizens complain that educators are preoccupied with their own agendas and don't address public concerns about discipline and teaching the basics. This lack of responsiveness is part of what convinces people that the public schools aren't really theirs. The relationship citizens have — or don't have — with schools seems to affect the way they view them.

There are other reasons that people are moving away from public schools. While Americans still cling to the historic ideal that we should have schools open to all, the broad mandate that tied the schools to this and other social, economic, and political objectives seems to have lost its power to inspire broad commitment. People reason that, if the schools can't help individuals, they certainly can't help the larger community.

Surely another, and obvious, cause of the disconnect between schools and communities is that some schools don't have strong communities to relate to in the first place. Communities vary in civic spirit and vitality, and schools may not have much to connect with if they are located in an area where people's jobs and associations are elsewhere. How can schools serve a community's general interests if those interests haven't been established? Even districts or cities with rich civic histories may neglect to reaffirm public purposes, which must be reaffirmed constantly in order to remain legitimate. Because demographics change so frequently, yesterday's city may not be today's. While we recognize the necessity for a community response to the web of problems affecting education, creating a community that can pull together poses a substantial challenge.

On the basis of what we have heard from teachers and administrators, I think other obstacles to a better relationship between citizens and schools grow out of the unhappy experiences these educators have had with what they see as "the public." Educators complain that they are often captives of externally imposed reforms, with little or no voice. They are wary, and not without reason. Battered by interest groups, administrators become quite guarded, saying, in effect, "You can't just pull a group of people together from the community to tell educators what to do." They worry that citizens want to be involved in what they see as staff and faculty decisions. Educators also frequently equate the public with parents. And, while involving parents is essential, they are only a third of the citizenry.

In light of these feelings, it's no wonder that those trying to change schools sometimes give what one reporter described as lip service to public involvement. It's no wonder that reforms often fail, divided within by disputes between educators and other key actors and besieged without by angry interest groups.[5] It's no wonder that, when educators talk about public engagement or community involvement, all they mean is using more effective ways of telling people what's good for them.

Given these circumstances, reclaiming the public schools would seem to be a responsibility that the public has to assume — although it would be a mistake to exclude educators.[6] I am saying that fundamental change has to start with the public and within the community if it is to be effective against the structural impediments in school systems that tend to block that change. It is also unlikely that schools will change unless communities change, unless citizens increase their capacity to band together and act together.

I am arguing, as well, that there isn't any single reform that will do for all time. As I see it, schools will always have to adapt to new circumstances and challenges. Improvement must be habitual, so schools have to have the ability to keep on changing. The capacity for continuous adaptation is the mark of healthy people and healthy institutions. I am not suggesting that all reforms are likely to fail; some have made significant improvements in the curriculum and administrative organization of schools. I am talking about something else — about an enduring capacity or characteristic

---

5 Steve Farkas with Jean Johnson, *Divided Within, Besieged Without: The Politics of Education in Four American School Districts* (New York: Public Agenda Foundation for Kettering Foundation, 1993). While this study reports the failure of many recent reform efforts, it shouldn't be assumed that all reforms have been unsuccessful. Exceptional superintendents and principals, some academics, and citizen groups have sometimes had conspicuous success in changing particular schools. Yet even those reforms that are successful in achieving specific goals may not be building the kind of relationship with the public that increases the likelihood that reform will be ongoing.

6 This constitutes what Professor Ronald Heifetz calls a "Type III" problem, one that professionals can't remedy solely through their own resources. See Heifetz, *Leadership without Easy Answers* (Cambridge, Mass.: Harvard University Press, Belknap Press, 1994), pp. 74–86.

feature of schools, which I believe is rooted in the communities that surround them.[7]

Communities themselves have to have the capacity to keep on adapting, to act and keep on acting. Their ability to do that is directly related to the quality of their public life, the kind of life and relationships citizens have with other citizens. Some communities have a rich public life; that is, they have a diverse network of civic associations organized for public work, opportunities for making decisions together, and traditions of cooperation that allow people to band together effectively. Other communities don't.

Scholars who see the public as a society of citizens and analyze the way it operates, or who have studied a community's civil society, have found important processes and key structures that we usually miss.[8] So, in a book that puts so much emphasis on "the public" and "the community," I thought it essential to report on our best understanding of both. The fourth chapter gives more details on what makes public life vigorous and healthy and introduces a new paradigm for understanding our communities.

The character of public life may not strike you as relevant to what goes on in schools — but it is. There are any number of reasons why a healthy public life is essential to good schools. Two come immediately to mind. Strong communities, with people banded and pulling together, are our last line of defense against the breakdown of families and society. And they are also an essential source of "social capital," a necessary form of reinforcement from outside the school that encourages students to learn.[9]

Focusing on the health of a community's public life (or what is sometimes called the civil part of society) gives us another way to think

---

7 See Václav Havel's March 31, 1995, address at Victoria University in Wellington, New Zealand, reprinted in *New York Review of Books* 22 (June 22, 1995): 36–37. Here, Havel explains how he came (by way of Karl Popper's criticism of holistic social engineering) to see continuous incremental adaptation as the most desirable approach to ameliorating world problems.

8 These scholars include Robert Putnam at Harvard University, Vaughn Grisham at the University of Mississippi, and Douglass North at Washington University, St. Louis. Their studies are cited elsewhere.

9 James S. Coleman and Thomas Hoffer, *Public and Private High Schools: The Impact of Communities* (New York: Basic Books, 1987), pp. 221–233.

about "the public." This perspective keeps us from equating the public with individuals, an audience, or even activists in interest groups; it directs our attention to the nature of the society in which citizens are embedded.

Because we have a different concept of the public or community, the strategy that follows from our research is quite different from the typical strategy for marshaling public support or increasing community involvement, which usually centers on enlisting key civic leaders and holding hearings for interested citizens, primarily for the purpose of winning support for schools. The public-first strategy we have in mind would work the other side of the street, actually deriving the mission for education from the purposes of the community. We think that schools as well as all other educational institutions should get their charters by "contracting" to reach public objectives. Standards or goals should be based on and directly related to community purposes rather than just professional criteria.

Our advice would be to start with the community or public, that is, to concentrate first on the community and its concerns rather than on the schools and their goals. We believe that schools are best understood as means to the broader educational objectives of a community and that well-intentioned reforms often reverse this natural order, treating the community as a means to ends dictated by schools. In effect, we propose retracing the steps that brought the public schools into being in the first place.

An obvious question: Are Americans interested in building stronger communities and regaining "ownership" of their schools? We have found that, although uncertain of what steps to take, many people are willing to act — if they can see a possibility of making a difference. The primary purpose of the foundation's research is to develop materials citizens can use in order to make such a difference. For instance, Kettering is preparing issue books or guides for making difficult choices on community and educational issues, which are similar to the National Issues Forums (NIF) books. We think that learning to make choices together about how to act is an essential part of working together as a community.

As I end this introductory chapter, I would like to return to what I said earlier: the public is slipping away from the public schools, and no one seems to be paying much attention. If the relationship between citizens and what are supposedly *their* schools is weak, fragile, and in disrepair, the first thing we need to do is not weaken it further. If the supports for a bridge have deteriorated, you don't keep driving eighteen-wheelers over it.

Today, news stories about education are framed largely around controversies over financing, the quality of instruction, and the efficiency of administration — punctuated with dramatic accounts of drugs and violence in the schools. If these stories are a barometer, the key actors in education aren't paying attention to the relationship between the public and the schools or to what has happened to the mandate for public education. Headlines typically describe the latest curriculum reform, a reorganization that consolidates local boards, or a school's prediction of dire consequences if still another funding levy fails. Though all are legitimate reports, framing the coverage around these controversies misses the story behind the story. Are some of the solutions to problems of finance, equity, quality, and efficiency putting even more distance between the public and the schools? Is the debate over these issues itself driving citizens away? Our research suggests that people find the discussion of reform and reorganization too technical to be coherent, too removed from their concerns to be relevant.

If the schools are losing the public, as the research suggests, or if "public" schools mean little more today than schools paid for by taxes and controlled by boards of citizens, then no plan for reform or reorganization should be attempted without looking at its impact on what appears to be a very fragile relationship linking the public and the schools. Whatever its merits, any arrangement that makes our schools less public will have serious consequences — not only for schools but for an entire country that was organized around the expectation that there would always be public education to "complete the great work of the American Revolution."

Who should assess the public impact of reform and reorganization? Why not the public?

CHAPTER 2

INDICATIONS OF
A DISCONNECT

To sum up what I've just said, as much as Americans feel a sense of duty to support public schools, they are torn and ambivalent, and many have begun moving away from them, in spirit if not in fact. The obvious reasons have already been noted. People believe school systems are too plagued by disorder and hamstrung by social problems to provide a good education. The quality of instruction is a major concern; people don't think the schools are teaching the basics.[1] Of course, not everyone feels this way. Some of the focus group participants said their schools were quite good. Yet, when pressed by others, they admitted that the high quality was probably a function of some special or exceptional circumstance — a good

---

1   The lack of confidence in public schools should be no surprise — most of our major institutions have lost standing with the public. From 1973 to 1993, the proportion of Americans indicating confidence in educational institutions dropped from 37 to 22 percent, while the proportion of those with little confidence rose from 8 to 18 percent. Everyone knows about loss of faith in government, but many other institutions experienced a similar decline in confidence, even organized religion, down from 35 to 23 percent. See National Opinion Research Center, "Public Opinion and Demographic Report: Confidence in Institutions," *American Enterprise* 4 (November 1993): 94–95.

neighborhood, the added resources of a "magnet" school. Even more disturbing, Americans don't believe there is much possibility of changing the situation, because the problems of the schools seem to grow out of deeper problems in our society — a breakdown of the family and norms of behavior.

We hear the public's distress echoed in the frustrations of educators. Teachers know all about social problems and how they invade their classrooms. As one in Houston reported, "I spend 60 percent of my time on discipline, 20 percent on filing, and, if I am lucky, I have 20 percent left for instruction."[2]

More serious than the loss of confidence, the historic tie between the public and the public schools appears to be weakening, as people who would like to stand by the schools decide that they no longer can   or should. Even among those happy with the public school their children attend, their allegiance is usually to that particular institution more than to the concept of public education. When given the opportunity to receive a "check" to send their children to private school, most parents — including those who spoke relatively positively about their public schools — chose that option.[3]

What can be done to reconnect the public to its schools? It's not simply that the schools need to be improved; the *relationship* between the schools and the community needs repair. Our research suggests that Americans are looking for a different way of working with educators; they want a relationship among equals. One woman from Massachusetts explained what her friends had in mind by using an analogy from business: "It's just like in a lot of industries. Where I work we're in what they call the team concept, and our business is running much better than it ever did when we had a hierarchy." A man in Maryland made a similar point when he said, "If we let the grass roots do more work, I think we'd be in good shape."[4]

---

2   Jim Mathews, conversation with author, 1995.

3   The Harwood Group, *Halfway Out the Door: Citizens Talk about Their Mandate for Public Schools* ([Dayton, Ohio]: Kettering Foundation, 1995).

4   Ibid., p. 19.

We won't begin to get at what has gone wrong in the relationship, however, until we are willing to think the unthinkable — that the public for public schools could be slipping away. Taking that perspective shifts our attention from the schools to the public they are intended to serve. As I have said, reforms have to start in and with the community if they are ever to move into the classroom. One experienced principal made the same point when he testified, "I learned that you can't do school reform inside the school."[5]

Why should we care whether public schools survive? Because it's more than the schools that are at risk: we're at risk of weakening every American institution and practice based on the premise that we would have a system of common schools to accomplish an army of public objectives. As one historian observed, our country has been able to allow individuals maximum freedom of action because we have had schools common to all to ensure social order; we deliberately opted for "anarchy with a schoolmaster."[6]

Novus Ordo Seclorum: Public Schools as a Means to Public Ends

Historically, "public" schools in America meant those that were the public's — that is, schools that were instruments of the people, chartered to do the important work of our country. Public schools were as much a foundation for American democracy as the Constitution and the Bill of Rights. We chose not to replicate the European state, which ordered society through strict control, relying instead on a school system that would create one nation out of diverse populations with long histories of conflict in their homelands.

But stability was not our highest ambition. America was founded to

5 Reported by Ann Hallett, Kettering Foundation meeting, minutes, 13 April 1995, Kettering Foundation, Dayton, Ohio, p. 3. In addition to The Harwood Group studies, see Jean Johnson et al., *Assignment Incomplete: The Unfinished Business of Education Reform* (New York: Public Agenda, 1995), pp. 12–13.

6 Rush Welter, *Popular Education and Democratic Thought in America* (New York: Columbia University Press, 1962), p. 49.

write a new chapter in human history — to create a "new secular order," an aspiration so fundamental that we stamped it on our most common currency, the one-dollar bill. Public schools were to be the agents of that aspiration, completing "the great work of the American Revolution." We reaffirmed that mandate in the Northwest Ordinance, written shortly after the Revolution: "Religion, morality and knowledge, being necessary to good government and the happiness of mankind, schools and the means of education, shall be forever encouraged." Ever since, at least until recently, schools have been seen as primary instruments of our country's objectives — from ensuring equity to defending the nation against the technological rival we once saw in the Soviet Union. The imperative of public purpose is as clear in the National Defense Education Act of 1958 as it was in the Northwest Ordinance of 1787.

Each era added its own directives to the mandate for public schools, which developed over time out of a wide-ranging debate among differing interests, eventually aligning around a national consensus that guided the country for the better part of two centuries. According to that mandate, in the process of giving each student a good education, schools were to:

- create and perpetuate a nation dedicated to particular principles, such as individual freedom and justice;
- develop a citizenry capable of self-government;
- ensure social order;
- equalize opportunity for all, so that the new nation would not perpetuate Europe's class divisions; and
- provide information and develop the skills essential to both individual economic enterprise and general prosperity.

To carry out these objectives, Americans not only built schools, they created libraries, museums, and a host of other educating institutions. The school was only one among many means of education.

Because schools and other educational institutions served larger public interests, all citizens were obliged to support them. That was the corollary implied in the mandate. Because public schools were our agents for creating the kind of country we wanted to live in, they merited our allegiance. That was the logic of the contract with the public, the basis for a special relationship between the citizenry and the schools. We acknowledged that relationship in the school buildings that sprang up all across America. Good schools were the measure of a good country and good communities.

That's what I grew up believing, in a family of schoolteachers; it's what I believed when I studied American history, and it's what I believed as Secretary of Health, Education, and Welfare on the bicentennial of our independence.

Schools Public in Character and Operation as Well as in Purpose

Our earliest schools were public in purpose but not in character or operation. Colonists brought with them a tradition of private academies, church schools, and apprenticeship education. We made our schools public in character and operation through a long struggle that took most of the nineteenth century. By its end, "public" schools in America had come to mean not only institutions paid for by public funds and controlled by citizen boards but also schools common and free to all citizens. To be sure, "free to all citizens" carried with it the nineteenth century's definitions of eligibility for citizenship, which specifically excluded African-Americans and Native Americans. Still, the ideals behind the promotion of public schools, particularly ideals like justice and equity, were a constant challenge to the prevailing restrictions.

That the state ought to pay for every citizen's education would have made little sense in the early nineteenth century. Even though Americans recognized the need to perpetuate learning, it was accepted practice to have proprietary schools for those who could afford them, with the state assuming responsibility only for children whose parents did not have adequate financial means. State schools were schools for the poor: they were pauper schools rather than public schools, reflecting a policy consistent with the prevailing view that education was primarily the responsibility of parents.

The idea that public schools should be common to everyone and paid for by everyone took decades to develop; it took root just before the middle of the nineteenth century, in response to a variety of social and economic changes. As suffrage spread and society became more diverse, the conscience of many Americans compelled them to pursue wide-ranging social reforms. And one of the principal institutions that reformers enlisted was the school.

The notion that schools could serve the well-being of all (that they were needed to make one nation of many people), along with the sense that there was an inconsistency between democratic ideals and state schools that served only the poor, eventually led to the creation of common schools. Different Americans had different reasons for subscribing to the common-school movement. Nonetheless, most, though not all, came to the conclusion that public schools were an essential public good and should be public in character, mirroring the highest ideals of a democratic nation.[7]

Early common schools were also public in that the citizenry was directly involved in their operation. People built the schools, controlled them through local trustees — not county school boards — and selected and housed their teachers. The community and the school were, in many ways, one. The community wasn't just "involved" with the school, the two were inseparable. As late as 1910, that was still the case. My grandfather, for example, began his teaching career by boarding in the homes of school trustees. In one of them, he met my grandmother.

A Twentieth-Century Amendment to the Contract

What happened to this history? Obviously, a great many things have changed in the course of this century. The relationship of the schools with the public has taken on a different cast as schools have reordered themselves

---

7 Lawrence A. Cremin, *The American Common School: An Historic Conception* (New York: Bureau of Publications, Teachers College, Columbia University, 1951).

to respond to demographic shifts and new social and legal pressures. The citizenry itself has changed, so that today's constituency for the schools isn't the same as it was 50 years ago. And the relationship has also changed as a result of what has happened to the management of schools. I am not suggesting that one set of forces has been more powerful than another, but I do feel a need to elaborate on the internal influences because they aren't well known.

While Americans didn't immediately abandon their contract with the public schools, they began to delegate much of the work of education to a new group of professionals. As the country became enthralled with what was believed to be a science of management and with the efficiency of professionally trained administrators, the public as a real force in the life of the schools was deliberately and systematically rooted out — all with the intention of removing political corruption. (The public was blamed for the popular support some corrupt politicians enjoyed.)

The closing decades of the nineteenth century saw the end of the Civil War, a series of major economic crises, and profound social unrest. These circumstances gave rise to a new generation of leaders, the Progressives, who promised more orderly change by relying on professional management of government and other institutions. Initially implementing some democratic reforms of their Populist predecessors, the Progressives eventually decided that citizens were unfit to govern and proclaimed themselves the surest guardians of the public interest.

In education, these trends played themselves out in initiatives to reduce direct public involvement and control. One of these efforts, known as Taylorism, attempted to increase school efficiency by applying the principles of a more "scientific" form of management. The centralization of rural schools and the professionalization of teaching would follow shortly.

The new guardians took direct aim at democratic control of schools. Typical of the group, Nicholas Murray Butler, president of Columbia University, maintained that the schools didn't really belong to the public but to their administrators. In a curious bit of reasoning, Butler argued that "a democracy is as much entitled as a monarchy to have its business well done."[8] I don't mean to imply that administrators, by themselves, set out to remove the public or that arguments like Butler's gave these officials total control of the schools (far from it!). Nonetheless, the country's enthusiasm for scientific or professional management led to building walls that kept citizens out. For example, inherently political issues in the educational debate became masked as scientific and technical considerations, which were not the province of the public.

Of course, many other forces have widened the gap between the public and its schools.[9] The point is not to lay blame on any one group but to note that the sources of the disconnect lie deep within our society's beliefs about efficiency and good management, beliefs that would not be challenged until the last of the twentieth century.

Failing Reforms: Divided Within and Besieged Without

I believe you will find that this history is not unrelated to what is happening to school reform today. Despite considerable energy, initial bursts of optimism, and abundant promises, a good many efforts to reform schools, though not all, are failing in the 1990s, "divided within and besieged without."[10] Key actors (educators, parents, business leaders, school board members) have been unable to overcome sharp differences over goals. Trapped in a web of suspicion, extreme partisanship, competitiveness, and poor communication, the leading participants have become the leading combatants, unable to reach any common ground. Other than these key actors, there has been no public, only factions or special interest groups

8   Nicholas Murray Butler, Speech to Chicago Merchants' Club, in *Public Schools and Their Administration: Addresses Delivered at the Fifty-ninth Meeting of the Merchants' Club of Chicago* (Chicago: Merchants' Club, 1906), p. 40.

9   One of the most frequently mentioned is transporting children to schools outside the areas where they live. The distant school is not a focal point for the children's community.

10 Steve Farkas with Jean Johnson, *Divided Within, Besieged Without: The Politics of Education in Four American School Districts* (New York: Public Agenda Foundation for Kettering Foundation, 1993). Of course, reforms don't all fail. The problem is that we don't seem to know how to sustain successes or move them from one school or area to another. Many successful reforms die when those who initiated them move on, and trying to imitate successful models doesn't seem to work.

organized to defeat any reforms that appear to threaten their turf. Even those closest to the school system have resorted to adversarial tactics. Parents, who might be expected to have an interest in the overall quality of education, have often pressured the schools in order to win personal concessions, not to change the system.

Katherine Boo, who reported on several leading initiatives in the *Washington Monthly*, came to much the same conclusion: reforms have floundered, disillusioning the communities that have undertaken them. Boo found one problem common to all the efforts: while the specific proposals were often superb, the reformers were unable to master the process of change.[11] Perhaps like football players intent on how they are going to run with a pass, these reformers didn't concentrate enough on catching the ball in the first place. In paying understandable attention to *what* they were going to change, some may have neglected the question of *how* to put the changes in place.

The reformers Boo wrote about didn't even involve parents. And, while paying lip service to the notion of citizen participation, they worked "doggedly to keep the masses from messing with their plans."[12] In these situations, the public doesn't have a seat at the table for discussions of school reform; and, as a result, there is no party that can incorporate special interests into a larger public interest or bring about a measure of accommodation among the key actors.

This approach to reform seems to take for granted that the long-standing commitment to public schools is still intact; that the contract remains in force and needs only to be invoked; that schools have merely to demonstrate legitimate needs in order for citizens to respond with financial support. It is assumed that the public can be rallied through the standard means of publicity and marketing: the buyers are out there waiting to be told the benefits of the product. Any trouble between school officials and the public is simply a failure to communicate.

---

11 Katherine Boo, "Reform School Confidential: What We Can Learn from Three of America's Boldest School Reforms," *Washington Monthly* 24 (October 1992): 17–24.

12 Ibid., p. 24.

The Lack of a Public for School Reform

These assumptions don't square with the way the public often responds to reform. In fact, Americans have an array of criticisms that explain why there is less of a public for school reform than is commonly imagined.[13]

Citizens may find discussions of reform incoherent and irrelevant. School officials, educational experts, and interest groups, who argue and point fingers, appear to be involved in a debate that lacks any promise of progress or possibility for real change. These key actors talk about discrete policy solutions and funding issues while ignoring public concerns. If reformers speak a technical rather than a public language, people feel that they don't really understand their problems. They say, in effect, "We are over here with the problems; the school reformers are over there with their solutions."

Even those with concerns that might be affected by reforms (parents, for example) don't feel welcome because, as they see it, their role is unacceptable to professionals. A 1992 survey found that, while nearly 60 percent of Americans thought parents and other members of the community should have more say in allocating funds and deciding the curriculum, less than 15 percent of administrators and only 26 percent of teachers shared this view.[14]

Consequently, citizens are frustrated by an absence of handles to take hold of the problems that worry them. This lack of agency evokes the kinds of feelings we have when we can't find a thermostat to control the temperature or the right knob to adjust a television set. People say such things as "I wouldn't know how to be involved, I really wouldn't." They may also feel that the things they are asked to do — providing more revenue or volunteering as aides — don't allow them to make a real difference because these measures are likely to be ineffective or "take too long." At most, people think they may help a particular child or a few

---

13 The Harwood Group, *How Citizens View Education: Their Public Concerns and Private Actions* ([Dayton, Ohio]: Kettering Foundation, 1993).

14 Steve Farkas, *Educational Reform: The Players and the Politics* (New York: Public Agenda Foundation for Kettering Foundation, 1992).

children through their own private actions; they see little opportunity for effective *public* action.[15] While this perception can be changed, it is currently an obstacle to a productive relationship between citizens and schools.

Lack of a sense of agency is compounded by a feeling that school systems are black holes, that any money they are given will be wasted through inefficient management. Those who might increase their financial support say they have to be convinced they won't be paying for more of the same.

Finally, and most serious of all, people may be unwilling to be involved in school reform because they don't believe that the public schools are really the *public's* schools. A man in a New Jersey inner city, when asked who "owned" the local schools, said he wasn't sure which level of government had jurisdiction. But he was certain that the schools didn't belong to his community; they were not, he said with conviction, "our schools."[16]

Taken together, these factors isolate the public schools from the public even as the schools try to reform themselves. School systems appear to be walled off as formal, quasi-governmental institutions rather than public agencies embedded in a rich civic network.

What Americans Want Today

Despite all that separates the public from the public schools, Americans are reluctant to abandon them; they aren't willing to do without them and still describe them as important. But to whom, and for what purpose?

Our research found that people didn't talk voluntarily about public schools playing any role beyond preparing their own individual children for the future. As a man in Baltimore said, the schools should teach "the basic essentials that are going to get [my child] through life." People from Atlanta to Denver defined the basics as reading, writing, and arithmetic. Although they mentioned teaching interpersonal skills needed to "fit into"

---

15 The Harwood Group, *How Citizens View Education,* pp. 28–31.

16 Reported by a member of a Teachers College, Columbia University, research team that conducted a study of education in Newark for the Kettering Foundation in 1985–1986.

society and social norms, like respect for others, this translated into helping a child grow up and become a better person. The central purpose of schooling is "to better *your* life, to better *your* position in life." When asked specifically about broader mandates for the schools, such as building a competitive work force, people said that these objectives are best met by concentrating on individuals and their development, that if each child gets a sound basic education society will reap the benefits. A nation is the product of its people, Americans reason.[17]

While we have always placed a premium on educating the individual, the corollary mandate, the one about creating a new social order or completing the great work of the American Revolution through schools, seems to have moved to the back of people's minds. It takes some prompting to get Americans to recall it, and they often find it difficult to talk about once they do. Some doubt that such a mandate ever really existed. Certainly no one is passing legislation these days with sentiments like those in the Northwest Ordinance.

Mandates from the community as a whole or the public at large, mandates that make a claim on Americans whether or not they have children who benefit directly from schools, no longer seem to be compelling. People don't base their actions on them; they don't see how the schools can serve any larger purposes if they can't even deliver on the basics. And parents, worried that their children won't get what they need from the schools, aren't inclined to be concerned with anything else. The operative mandate has narrowed to what people consider the minimum, that is, maintaining discipline and teaching the essentials. Americans today don't see the public schools as agents for creating a better society — ironically, at the very time they despair over the state of the present social order.

Has a Private Mandate Replaced the Public One?

Americans may insist on keeping a public school system out of a sense of tradition (we have always had public schools) and because of the

---

17 The Harwood Group, *Halfway Out the Door,* pp. 8–10.

importance they place on giving all youngsters an opportunity to better themselves. A reason shared by many was implied by the question of a man in Boston: "If you didn't have public schools, where would the children go if they couldn't afford to go to private school?"[18] Americans believe children must have a chance to improve themselves, irrespective of their financial circumstances.

Does this suggest that we are moving back to the arrangement of the early 1830s, when public schools were schools for the poor? Are public schools going to become facilities important to have, open to all, serving individual needs rather than broad social purposes, and a last resort for those who have no alternative? If people are saying that we should have schools "for the masses" but "I don't want to send my kids there and you shouldn't either," we may end up with a very different kind of public school system from the one we have had for most of our history.

Faced with Hard Choices

Americans might reject this interpretation of what they are saying. The people we interviewed in the research expressed deep concern about what would happen if the country turned away from the public schools. They feared it would widen the gap between haves and have-nots, so they were skeptical of vouchers or letting market forces have full sway. These strategies, one woman observed, "sound like the rich getting richer and the poor getting poorer." People are also well aware that the public school has been one of the few American institutions where individuals of diverse backgrounds have come together. That realization, more than anything else, generates support for public education.[19] Sentiments like these echo the original public mandate, however faintly.

Still, even if we haven't moved back to the 1830s, we are struggling with the same issue: Can we have schools common and free to all and, at the same time, get what is best for children? Whatever Americans may have decided over a century ago, that decision doesn't hold today. The question

18 Ibid., p. 4.
19 Ibid., p 5.

is very much open, and the choice is both real and difficult.

Which way the decision will go is impossible to predict at this point. But, as push comes to shove in the 1990s, it appears that many would sacrifice the unique benefits of a public school system and risk isolating children in homogeneous private or home schools in order to give them a good education. As The Harwood Group reported, Americans are more than halfway out the schoolhouse door. When citizens around the country were asked whether they would prefer public schools as they are to what they perceive private schools to offer, a virtual chorus said they would take their children out of public school if they had that option. People often feel trapped in the public schools. "Low-income people can't move," explained a woman in Chicago; "We are in such a hopeless situation right now," a Boston woman lamented. Even those who think the public schools are not all bad said that where their children would wind up was just the luck of the draw.[20] Echoing those interviewed in the study, a California journalist made the same point: "If I had to choose, I think most children would be better off with no public schools at all than with the ones we have now."[21]

Looking for a Different Relationship

The attraction of private schools is telling. Americans imagine them to be what public schools should be but aren't. For example, many genuinely fear for their children's safety in public schools and see private institutions as havens of discipline.

One of the most appealing features may be the relationship between these schools and their constituents. Parents, grandparents, alumni, and even the parents of alumni are actively encouraged to become involved. Interestingly, what people who like a particular public school say they like most is their close association with it. Taking part in the life of a school seems to be linked to a perception that the school is a good one. As one person said, when asked about why he believed in public schools, "[My

20 Ibid., pp. 13–15.
21 Linda Seebach, "Government Runs Schools No Better Than It Runs Churches," *Dayton Daily News,* 19 January 1995, p. 15A.

kids] are going to an excellent school, *and I am involved with it.*"[22]

Unfortunately, many parents of public school students wouldn't say that.[23] The mother of a sixth grader told of her frustration that she can't occasionally have lunch with her child in the cafeteria or deliver a last-minute message on the playground at recess — she must go through "channels." Contrast that with someone else's memories of his own school days, when children were on their best behavior because they knew their parents were welcome to drop by the school at any time — and often did.

If people don't think the schools are theirs, it's no wonder they don't feel at home in them. Ironically, visitation days and special occasions to open the doors only emphasize the distance between the public and the schools. Visitors are invariably seen as guests, who don't really belong in the hallways. Teachers say they have been burned by so many bad experiences with what they think of as "the public" that they are reluctant to welcome citizens. They sometimes see their classrooms like operating rooms; when community groups ask to visit them, they respond that "just anybody shouldn't be allowed in."

Lack of hands-on or "in-the-hallways" ties between citizens (not just parents) and the schools may go a long way in explaining why the relationship has soured. Our research has shown that people approach problems asking whether they can do anything that could make a difference. If the answer is no, if they can't find anything to get their hands on, they lose interest. Being assured that someone else is doing something doesn't substitute for a personal role. Getting our hands on a problem prompts a sense that we *might* make a difference. While no one expects complete success, progress becomes imaginable. Under those

---

22 The Harwood Group, *Halfway Out the Door,* p. 14. For more on the effects of relationships on perceptions, see Ernest G. S. Noack, "The Satisfaction of Parents with Their Community Schools as a Measure of Effectiveness of the Decentralization of a School System," *Journal of Educational Research* 65 (April 1972): 355–356.

23 This is not to deny that many people, particularly parents, are deeply involved with schools as volunteers. Yet even the highly active parents give themselves low marks for their participation in the life of the school, as contrasted with their efforts in connection with their children's homework. See Institute for Educational Leadership, "Survey of Parent Involvement" (Institute for Educational Leadership, Washington, D.C., 1995, photocopied).

circumstances, negative perceptions become more positive.[24]

To sum up, once strong and direct ties between the citizenry and the schools seem to have become weak and distant. As one researcher reported, "The public and the schools haven't gotten a divorce, but they are definitely separated."[25] The situation resembles the sad case of a 20-year marriage in which the husband no longer sees his wife as his soul mate but thinks of her as his housekeeper. And the wife no longer sees her husband as the man of her dreams but merely as the breadwinner. Though still married, they are ready to live apart. Though they remain under the same roof, their association is punctuated by criticism and countercriticism. The terms of the relationship have changed.

It is difficult to avoid the impression that the public schools are seen today like public transportation or even like the automatic bank teller on the corner, more *in* the community than *of* it. The schools aren't all of *us* as a community doing our job, they are merely hired hands doing a job *for* us.

It is tempting to believe that, if schools could successfully address the discipline problem or if they returned to teaching the basics, people would see them differently. Yet, as many have observed, schools can't change on their own because the forces disrupting them come from outside, not inside, the classroom. Americans understand very well that the schools are a microcosm of our society. Furthermore, improving the schools, even if that were possible in the present circumstances, would not necessarily rebuild their relationship with the public.

Retracing Our Steps

What would rebuild that relationship? Our history and Kettering research suggest that in order to reconnect the public with the schools we may have to retrace our steps, going back through the process that led to their creation. As I said in the last chapter, that would require starting with the public rather than the schools.

24 The Harwood Group, *Meaningful Chaos: How People Form Relationships with Public Concerns* (Dayton, Ohio: Kettering Foundation, 1993).

25 John Creighton, conversation with author, 1995.

Remember that when I refer to "the public" I don't mean individuals, an audience, or a constituency; I mean citizens, people who might engage one another in taking responsibility for their common problems and act together to improve their common future. I am not thinking of saints or key leaders in a community, and I don't limit the definition to parents of school-age children. I have in mind busy, worried, preoccupied people of all kinds, who are joined together as a society of citizens.

What was it that created an American public out of the different groups who settled this country? What led to the American commitment to public education and public schools? Although these are the subjects of the remainder of this book, I want to give you the gist of our hypothesis about reconstituting publics and reaffirming educational mandates or imperatives. Publics, or political communities, form around a very basic question: What kind of community do we want to be? Of course, no one asks such an abstract question, and there is never one general answer. We respond through a series of specific choices we make about how to create a productive economy, structure government, take care of those unable to work, raise taxes, and so on. Choices are crucial, and how we make them — particularly who is involved in making them — determines whether and what kind of public is formed. The point is that the most fundamental choices are about community. Other decisions, such as those about agencies within communities — schools or local governments, for example — are driven by those primary choices.

School issues are especially prone to be treated in isolation from other relevant community concerns, remaining narrowly focused on professional considerations. Debates over the curriculum or school discipline can be badly misdirected. A question about the curriculum may be a surrogate for a question about economic strategies, while a question about discipline in the schools may really be part of a larger question about how to maintain order in the community. Issues that are misframed this way can't be resolved because the stakeholders aren't all at the table. Issues that we might be tempted to see simply as problems within schools need to be reframed to embrace the larger context of community concerns.

Decisions about the kind of community we want to be invariably lead us to thinking about the means we are going to use to become such a community. Some of those means will be political, involving laws and regulations that encourage certain behaviors and prohibit others. Some will surely be educational, because we can't become all we want to be solely through legislation. Education, which is considerably more than schooling, is a necessary means to accomplishing many of our most cherished public purposes, and it is from these that school mandates are derived. Moving from choices about our communities to determining the educational means needed to implement our decisions is part of what I mean by "retracing our steps." This process would set the stage for working out a new contract between the public and its schools, one grounded in a revitalized relationship.

Are Americans up to the challenge? Are we so absorbed in private pursuits ("bowling alone," as one study put it)[26] that we no longer have time for what people call "banding together"? It would be as foolish to ignore the trend to forsake public life for the presumed security of private safety as it would be to ignore the barriers separating the public from the schools. Still, the conviction that communities have to work together rings clear in the research. A rather quiet man from Portland, Oregon, who made few comments during a focus group session, spoke with obvious passion on this point. As his group was about to break up, he said, "We sit here and we criticize public schools — they're awful, they're no good." Then, with growing force in his voice, he asked, "But who the hell's going to change it?" He answered his own question: "We are. We're going to change it. In your life you've got to do something. Everybody's got to do something."[27]

We are learning more about the conditions that prompt people like this man to join together as a public and work together as a community. That is the subject of the next two chapters.

---

26 Robert D. Putnam, "Bowling Alone: America's Declining Social Capital," *Journal of Democracy* 6 (January 1995): 65–78.

27 The Harwood Group, *Halfway Out the Door*, p. 19.

CHAPTER 3

PUTTING THE PUBLIC BACK INTO PUBLIC EDUCATION

The last chapter suggested that we recharter our public schools by retracing our history through what I would call "public strategies." While it is obvious that we can't re-create the historical forces of the nineteenth century, we *can* use strategies based on the proposition that there must be a public before there can be public schools. Community development has to precede school reform. Reconstituting public life in our communities, strengthening our ties as citizens, can pave the way for *sustainable* school improvement, can endow schools with the capacity for continuous adjustment to new challenges.

Public strategies make sense if we think of schools as more than institutions, that is, as extensions of the community. As I see it, schools can't simply be institutions in our communities the way a distribution center for a chain of retail stores is in a community. Schools are meant to be an integral *part of* a community, so strengthening the public is actually strengthening the public schools.

If this is the case, as I believe it is, then it is reasonable to say that we have to look to our communities first if we are going to make fundamental changes in our school systems or develop their greater capacity for continuous improvement. Public strategies for rechartering schools are ways of reconnecting them to the purposes of a community. These purposes become the basis for contracts or charters in which communities commission schools to carry out certain mandates. Why is a commission, contract, or charter so important? Because schools acquire legitimacy when their objectives come from public mandates. That is, when people see that the schools are serving their purposes, they tend to see them as *their* schools. Our research suggests that, when schools have an active and explicit mandate from the public, they are more likely to be orderly and excellent and communities are more likely to be well served. Strategies for strengthening public life in a community should result in a greater capacity to act and to change, and schools in these communities, provided the ties are strong, should benefit from this same capacity. Ongoing improvement should be the norm.

"Public strategies" may sound like the popular phrase "community involvement," but they are not necessarily the same. Efforts to involve citizens, though well intentioned and sincere, sometimes unwittingly treat the public as a means to ends that educators have in mind. In talking to people about public participation, I realized that some see this as a technique whose effectiveness is judged by how well it helps schools reach their objectives. The public schools really are the *public's* schools, and the public's involvement is not by sufferance of the educational authorities. Citizens belong in the schools' hallways because they are *their* hallways. If they are given the impression that they are welcome to participate only if they can do something that educators think worthwhile, this puts the cart before the horse (i.e., treats citizens as means) and disconnects the public from the schools.

The public is not a means to the ends of educators, and people know it. They react adversely to many of the techniques used to involve them; though educators intend to empower, people feel manipulated. For example, the common practice of having the community discuss its needs, on the assumption that this will make people feel "involved" — while consultants and staff members develop curricular reforms based on long-held professional preferences — gives people the sense that educators are experimenting with their children and not listening to what they are saying. Researchers say practices like this have created a "legacy of mistrust."[1]

Public strategies, based on the proposition that the public "owns" the schools, are long-term strategies.[2] They can't promise the same quantifiable results that public relations techniques do: they may not help pass this month's levy or elect the best candidates to the board in next year's elections. They are also practices rather than tactics or how-to-do-it techniques. By "practices" I mean ways of relating and working together that have an intrinsic value; they express something that is important to us. The way we raise our children, for example, is a practice rather than a technique. Public practices, as distinct from family practices, have to do with the way we relate to one another in a community, such as the way we define our common interests or solve our common problems. They have to do with the way schools relate to communities, the way citizens relate to schools and schools to citizens. Public strategies change communities by restructuring relationships within them; they do that by affecting the practices of working together.

I will present public strategies as a series of steps, not because things happen in linear, step-by-step order, but because some things have to be in place before other things become possible. For that reason, I explain how a strong public is formed before describing practices that can help restructure the relationship between the public and the schools.

1   John Doble, telephone interview by Dana Marie Boswell and Kristin Lymburner, transcript, 28 August 1995, Kettering Foundation, Dayton, Ohio.

2   The feeling of people that they "own" the schools is not the same as local control of schools. The first is a communitywide perception; the second is a legal arrangement giving a group of educators and citizens authority over certain financial and curricular decisions. Citizens may actually be a minority in some local councils. Local control may grow out of a sense of public ownership, or it may simply be a particular form of control over schools that remain isolated from the community at large.

Step One: Reconstituting Publics

Because I have argued that the mandates linking schools to the community can come only from a public, I feel obliged to keep emphasizing what I think a public is as I move to an account of how a public comes into being. Earlier, I said that I was talking about a society of citizens, a diverse array of people who share certain problems or concerns and who are connected in ways that allow them to act together as they face them.

Being connected is the key. People in a shopping mall aren't a public because they aren't connected. They are just "the many," who have no public life. Publics exist by virtue of certain kinds of relationships citizens have with one another. So I think it is useful to talk about publicness as a particular characteristic of relationships rather than arguing about whether there is such a thing as a public.

What are public relationships like, and how are they different from other relationships? To begin with, they are associations we form with people who join us in common work and aren't the same as family ties or personal friendships. They are relationships with neighbors and even strangers who live near us. While ties to our mothers and fathers are fixed at birth, public relationships are constantly being formed, eroded, and re-formed. These relationships also have characteristic qualities: they are pragmatic as well as open and inclusive. Although we may not always like our fellow citizens personally, we may have to work with them in order to solve problems. Two leading civic activists in a small southern town had worked closely together for years. When one died, everybody said to the survivor, "You must have really liked Glen." "No," he responded, "I really hated the SOB, but we needed one another."

We carry on public relationships through particular kinds of conversations, in which we are constantly exploring options for action, through dialogue rather than debate. These relationships lead to a distinctive kind of action, to cooperative civic action that is complementary and mutually reinforcing.

A geographic community may or may not have these qualities of publicness; it may or may not have a public. Publics take time to form. Early Americans had to constitute themselves as a public before they could write the Constitution. More than a hundred years passed between the establishment of the first settlements and the confederation of the colonies into a nation. In fact, as Thomas Paine reminded his contemporaries, drafting the Constitution was itself a step in constituting a public. As the continent was settled, publics had to be formed in every town that sprang up. We have all seen that happen in Westerns, when townfolk overcome their paralysis and hire a sheriff to help them drive out the "bad guys." They stand with their new lawman on the main street to demonstrate their determination to bring order to the settlement. By sharing some purpose, these people cease to be simply a collection of individuals; they become a community and their relationships become public.

How Publics Form

We need to know as much as we can about how publics come into being — how busy, worried, preoccupied individuals become members of a public and take responsibility for what happens in their communities and schools.

Public relationships are formed in very specific ways. They emerge when people see connections between what is happening to them, on the one hand, and what is valuable to them, on the other. They form around a sense of common fate, interdependence, and overlapping purposes. They come alive in a willingness to take responsibility and act together (again, think of the Westerns).

A real-life example of public-forming occurred in the state of Washington around Lake Union, near downtown Seattle. Along the south shore of the lake is a sprawling collection of houseboats. Home to students, sailors, boatyard workers, poor folk, and retired radicals, this settlement was threatened in the early 1960s by environmentalists concerned about sewage discharge into the lake and developers seeking to acquire the lakefront for apartments. A public began to form when the owners of floating homes, rather than creating a special interest group to fight the environmentalists and developers, looked for a way to connect their interests to the interests of homeowners, businesses, and others living in the area. Environmentalists, houseboat owners, people who had homes on the shore, and storekeepers created a community around an effort to preserve the lake for their varied but interrelated interests. The houseboat owners paid for sewage lines, but this wasn't a concession forced through a legal settlement. Finding interrelated purposes had turned a group of people into a community, which has continued to exist well beyond the crisis that led to its formation.[3]

When I refer to a sense of interdependence and interrelated purposes, I know I am describing intangibles that may seem ideal, even miraculous. Yet our research suggests that these powerful feelings of community and public relationship grow out of tangible activities, which begin with the naming of problems and framing of issues.[4]

Naming Problems and Framing Issues in Public Terms: Who names the problems in a community and the names that are chosen — even the language that is used — are critically important. If experts name problems in technical terms, a great many people who should be providing leadership aren't going to become involved. Citizens usually have a different "take" on issues from that of experts or institutions. They respond to problems described in public language that is based on everyday experience and the things people consider most valuable. For example, many Americans are inclined to see stopping drug abuse as a family or community issue rather than simply a matter of enforcing the law or preventing drugs from entering the country. Naming the problem in legal terms shuts out those who see drug abuse every day in their neighborhoods and think of it as a

---

3   Harry C. Boyte, *Community Is Possible: Repairing America's Roots* (New York: Harper and Row, 1984), pp. 199–211.

4   The Harwood Group, *Meaningful Chaos: How People Form Relationships with Public Concerns* (Dayton, Ohio: Kettering Foundation, 1993).

problem of failed families, weak communities, and lack of economic opportunity.[5]

Naming problems in public terms also enables people to see them in ways that reflect not only their own interests but the interests of others. That builds a sense of shared fate; it is the first step in citizens taking responsibility for what happens to them as a community.

Naming problems in public terms can set off a chain reaction. Giving a problem a name and describing it to reflect the way families and communities experience it prompt people to think of things they can do to combat the threat. Problems can then be recast, or "framed," around various options for action. The issue of what to do about drug abuse can be framed around such approaches as urging young people "to just say no," or strengthening the community through projects like a neighborhood drug watch, or attacking root causes, like the lack of jobs. Framing issues this way, laying out all the options, helps people get a handle on problems that might otherwise overwhelm them.

Making Public Choices through a Deliberative Dialogue: Naming problems and framing issues in public terms set the stage for the next critical step in forming public relationships — making choices together so people can act together. At a recent town meeting in Grand Rapids, a mother who had lost two sons to random violence said simply but with conviction, "We have to band together to stop the killing." Communities can't band together, however, unless they can make decisions about the purposes and direction of action, which are always difficult. Conflicts inevitably arise because a great many things are valuable to us, and we have no way of being certain which of our concerns should guide our decisions about how to act. In dealing with an issue like drug abuse, we place a

5   Using the drug problem as an example has the advantage of illustrating the difference between the way experts or professionals may approach an issue and the way citizens experience it. The disadvantage is that the example seems to suggest that citizens should make choices about means and not ends. Actually, the most important decisions are about objectives, purposes, and directions. The details of implementation are usually the province of professionals. In the case of the drug issue, however, a public consensus on the objective already exists: there is little controversy over whether we need to combat the abuse of street drugs like crack.

premium on families, and so we are tempted to use our resources to strengthen them. But we also believe discipline and order are valuable, and that prompts us to use our resources to strengthen the police force and build prisons in order to get drug pushers off the streets.

Making these kinds of difficult choices requires a deliberative dialogue, which is different from popular expression (sounding off), information gathering, or debate. Deliberation explores several basic questions: What is valuable to us when we think about a particular problem? What are the costs and consequences of the various options for acting on that problem? What are the tough choices that make the decision so difficult? The final question can take a variety of forms: Where do we want this policy to take us? What are we willing to do to solve the problem? What trade-offs are we willing (or unwilling) to make? In responding to these questions, people are moving toward a decision, not just exchanging ideas. They have to "work through" conflicts over which of the many things that are valuable to them should inform their actions. People don't have to be in complete agreement, but they do have to look for a general direction or range of actions they can live with.

To deliberate, people have to talk citizen-to-citizen and face-to-face rather than simply listening to expert presentations. They have to examine a wide variety of perspectives and weigh the pros and cons of every option. That is what deliberation is — carefully weighing options against what is truly valuable.

Deliberation is a process of decision making that is tied to action. While it doesn't necessarily result in agreement, it can produce a general sense of direction and reveal shared or interrelated purposes. These "products" create a feeling of possibility, which generates civic energy for implementing decisions. By watching thousands of National Issues Forums, convened by civic and educational organizations across the country, the Kettering Foundation has been able to see how deliberative dialogue works.[6] Its first

---

6 National Issues Forums (NIF) provide opportunities for citizens across the nation to gather and deliberate on the most challenging issues of the day. The forums are organized by thousands of civic, service, and religious organizations, as well as by libraries, high schools, and colleges. Each year since

effect is to change people by changing their attitudes. Although forum participants may not alter their own positions on an issue, they may change their opinions of others' opinions. Deliberation allows us to "take in" other people's experiences. As we internalize their views, we are changed, our perceptions of others are changed, and we see possibilities for acting together that we hadn't seen before.[7]

Deliberation also affects the way people see the issues themselves. Take economic development programs, for example, which often begin with an effort to attract new industries to a given area. Cities with this objective define their problem initially as a need for jobs. But later, after much deliberation, some come to see their economic situation in a different light. What they really have to work on, they decide, is creating prosperity, not simply adding jobs (which may or may not bring prosperity). This redefinition of the issue has led some cities to develop broad strategies for creating "entrepreneurial economies": they draw on existing resources to create a variety of new businesses that fill niches in what is now an international economy.

Modification of these two key perceptions — of one another and of the problem — unlocks the sense of possibility that is the driving force behind change. People don't require a guarantee that what they do will be successful. They will join in civic action if they understand clearly how a problem affects what they care about, if they see that there is something they may be able to do about it, and if they discover that there are others

---

1981, Kettering and Public Agenda have prepared NIF books designed to stimulate serious deliberation on three different issues of national concern — poverty, health care, national security, the drug crisis, and the environment, among others.

7   For a more complete account of the effects of public deliberation, see John Doble Research Associates, *The Story of NIF: The Effects of Deliberation* (Dayton, Ohio: Kettering Foundation, 1996), Steve Farkas and Will Friedman, with Ali Bers, *The Public's Capacity for Deliberation* (New York: Public Agenda for Kettering Foundation, 1996), and John Gastil, Gina Adam, and Hank Jenkins-Smith, *A Builder's Guide to Public Deliberation: An Executive Summary of "Understanding Public Deliberation"* (Albuquerque: Institute for Public Policy, University of New Mexico, for Kettering Foundation, 1995).

who will work with them.[8] That is how political will is generated.

Difficult decisions about how to act are made in stages, never all at once. We usually begin by blaming the difficulties on others before working through the emotions provoked by having to face unpleasant costs and consequences.[9] Working through an issue takes a long time, goes on in many different settings, and moves in fits and starts. Conversations may begin as friendly backyard exchanges long before they become seriously deliberative. Typically, we start talking about personal concerns and then try to find out whether anyone else shares our worries. For example, one public-forming exchange began with neighbors talking about the drug paraphernalia they found alongside the streets.[10] Informal conversations may turn into a larger dialogue at a neighborhood gathering. Later, a town meeting may be held on the issue. Months, even years, of deliberation may pass before we determine whether and how to act.

Taking Public Action: In the final analysis, publics and public relationships are created through the common work of public action. Public action isn't the same as the action of special interest groups; it is comprehensive and inclusive rather than categorical. And it isn't the same as governmental or institutional action, which is uniform, linear, and usually coordinated by some administrative agency. The fire department lays out rules for exiting a building safely. It sends an inspector around from time to time to supervise a fire drill. The interactions are vertical — from officials down to citizens or, in some cases, from citizens up to officials.

Public action isn't linear, beginning at one point and ending at another. It is an organic, ever repeating collection of efforts, richly diverse and involving many people. Neighbors working together to restore a park — pitching in to clean up trash, plant trees, or build benches — is an example

---

8   The Harwood Group, *Meaningful Chaos,* pp. 11-14, 31-34.

9   Daniel Yankelovich, *Coming to Public Judgment: Making Democracy Work in a Complex World* (Syracuse, N. Y.: Syracuse University Press, 1991).

10 The Harwood Group, *Meaningful Chaos,* pp. 11–12.

of public action. The interactions are horizontal — shoulder-to-shoulder, citizen-to-citizen. Public action isn't the product of an administrative plan, nor is it spontaneous or magical. It grows out of deliberation, which, if it goes well, results in a sense of direction. We are able to identify where interests overlap and where purposes can be joined.

Think of a community faced with the problem of growing vandalism. As people deliberate over what to do, they may not agree on any one solution, but they can develop a shared sense that cleaning and fixing up neighborhoods might help. Several neighborhood groups may meet afterward, with residents volunteering to show up at local parks the following Saturday. Once people have a common sense of direction and have made a commitment to act, they are able to take on all kinds of community projects.

Public action isn't a substitute for carefully planned actions by governmental or nongovernmental organizations, although it has certain qualities that other forms of action lack. Economists would say that its transaction costs are lower because, even though it requires a degree of coordination (everyone can't show up at the park to mow grass and pick up trash), it isn't administratively regulated. When people have overlapping purposes, their diverse efforts tend to mesh, complementing and reinforcing one another.

Cities and towns where there is little public action and where everything that is done has to be highly organized and planned in detail can miss the initiative and inventiveness that allow them to be optimally effective. What's more, institutional action often fails to produce results when it isn't reinforced by public action. Consider the way a good neighborhood-watch program helps a police department do its job. Fred Smith, who retired three years ago from the machine-tool shop, devotes Monday afternoons to checking the street from his front porch (until time for Monday-night football). Once everyone is home from work, the Joneses and the Turners walk together after supper for company, to exercise and, not incidentally, to establish a presence on the block.

Because official interactions are vertical while public interactions run the other way, they can support each other. When the two are woven together, as with threads, the result is the strong "whole cloth" of community action. If it were not for the threads crossing one another in the fabric of our clothes, our elbows would come through our shirtsleeves.

Judging Results Publicly: Once formed, publics must be constantly re-formed. Public relationships, like all other human relationships, can break down unless they are conscientiously maintained. Ironically, these relationships often collapse at the end of major civic projects because of the way the results are evaluated. Traditional methods of measuring outcomes can undermine the very thing that makes for success — an involved and responsible citizenry. They can also cause us to miss rich opportunities for civic learning, which should be a part of judging results.

We insist on knowing the results of our work because we want to be successful — as well we should. If we didn't insist on this, efforts to change communities would degenerate into the worst kind of therapy: warm, fuzzy feelings of momentary comfort. We usually ask professionals to evaluate projects by "scientific" means, or we use quantitative methods ourselves to see whether we have more or less of certain things. In both cases, the process unintentionally pushes the citizens of a community to the sidelines and diminishes their sense of ownership and responsibility.

Being successful over the long term requires an active public, one involved in an ongoing process of making judgments about whether the results a community is getting from its efforts are consistent with what is truly valuable to its citizens. That is how a community develops the capacity for continuous adaptation and ongoing improvement. What I am proposing would give us a more public kind of accountability, with citizens directly involved in assembling and weighing the evidence of accomplishment, evidence that included their own experiences. The public would evaluate itself rather than merely receive reports of what institutions and agencies had done.

A Public Is Not the Same as a Persuaded Populace

In order to be as clear as I can about what I mean by a "public" and "public-forming," I have to make one additional distinction. Others have used phrases like "creating a public" to mean generating popular support for a particular message or cause. I would describe a public as an *engaged* citizenry, in order to distinguish it from a *persuaded* populace.

Public relations efforts can persuade people and gather support for good causes, but they can't create genuine publics. Publics are formed when people decide, among themselves, to live and act in certain ways. Making these decisions together gives their choices legitimacy and moral force. If their choices are the result of the political equivalent of sales pressure, they lack authenticity. Being sold on what someone else has decided doesn't have the same moral weight; it doesn't promote the deep sense of responsibility that forms publics. When people respond to a message rather than to one another, they aren't building public relationships. Conventional public relations doesn't provide for the public decision making that's required to create an engaged citizenry.

Obviously, people in positions of authority, such as heads of institutions, have to develop proposals and "sell" them as best they can. That is as it should be, and sometimes we "buy" what is being sold. But do we "own" it? The unhappy answer is: not always. We may not take responsibility for the outcome of a course of action we have bought, preferring to blame the "manufacturers" (i.e., those in authority) for anything that goes wrong. We take more responsibility for what we have participated in choosing than for what we have been sold.

I am certainly not suggesting that persuasion is wrong. Still, while any political action requires that someone take the initiative, it doesn't follow that all citizens have to do is sit back and wait to be persuaded. People have to become engaged in making up their own minds about their community's directions and purposes.[11]

---

11 For a more detailed discussion of the process of forming publics, see David Mathews, *Community Politics,* rev. ed. (Dayton, Ohio: Kettering Foundation, [1995]).

Step Two: Reaffirming Educational Imperatives

Before turning to a discussion of reconnecting the public with the schools, I should report on what we have learned about the role education plays in the community. A community has to consider which of its objectives require education and which institutions can provide that education before it is ready to talk about what schools should do. Notice that I am intentionally distinguishing education from schools or schooling, for reasons that I'll get to shortly.

Historically, communities educated long before they had schools; the need for systematic instruction eventually led to their creating specialized institutions to provide schooling. So, in retracing the steps that led to the public school, it makes sense to reaffirm educational imperatives first.

Publics or communities are naturally and necessarily educative. Educating, at its root, connotes shaping, forming, and fashioning so as to improve. To educate is to lead or bring forward, as well as to draw out. Creating a good community requires a lot of shaping and bringing forward: new practices have to be introduced, new skills learned, new relationships developed. All of that calls for education.

Our history abounds in examples of using education to create a better life for a community. When the colonists wanted to prevent the English social-class system from replicating itself in the New World, their workingmen's associations used both educational and political means to ensure that workers wouldn't be second-class citizens. These associations not only championed schools, they created a variety of other educating institutions — mechanics' institutes, reading rooms, libraries — where laborers could improve their minds and their skills.[12] In our own century, the federal government emphasized mathematics and science education in the 1950s as part of a strategy of national defense against technological advances by Communist-bloc countries. And we created Freedom Schools to teach citizenship in the 1960s as part of a strategy to expand civil rights.

---

12 Rush Welter, *Popular Education and Democratic Thought in America* (New York: Columbia University Press, 1962), p. 49.

Different Reactions to "Education" and "Schools"

While Americans initially tend to equate education with schools, they soon go on to say that education is much more than schooling. Asked to describe where education occurs, people mention churches, books, field trips, television, zoos, youth organizations, libraries, museums and, most of all, jobs. They say that what they learn from these "educators" is much like what they learn in schools: skills and values, history and foreign languages, an understanding of other cultures.[13]

Our research found, however, that the words "education" and "schools" prompted very different reactions, reactions colored with considerable emotion. When people were asked what first came to mind when they heard each of them, "schools" recalled unhappy experiences; people associated schools with violence, poorly paid teachers, principals who won't fire incompetent teachers, the pill, condoms, teen pregnancy. The word "education," on the other hand, suggested "knowledge, opportunity, and experience."[14]

One reason for these quite different reactions may be that people think they can educate, whereas they don't think they can provide much schooling. Americans usually feel very connected to education. Baton Rouge, a city of nearly 300,000 on the Mississippi River, was the site of a focus group whose 12 randomly selected members were asked how they educated others. Four of the twelve held college degrees, while the same number had not gone beyond high school. The group included men and women of different ages, races, and financial circumstances. Diverse as their experiences had been, none had any difficulty giving example after example of direct and meaningful ways in which they educated — through literacy programs, through their churches, and through a variety of community projects.[15]

---

13 John Doble Research Associates, "Summaries of Five Research Projects" (Kettering Foundation, Dayton, Ohio, April 1995, photocopied), p. 4.

14 Ibid., p. 3.

15 John Doble, memorandum to Kettering Foundation's Comprehensive Educational Resources Project Work Group, 13 April 1992, Kettering Foundation, Dayton, Ohio.

Education Is Everyone's Responsibility

"Education is important to everything," people say; and that conclusion leads them to add that "education is everyone's responsibility." Americans refuse to pin the burden of solving the problems of education solely on the schools. "There are so many things that flow into this one subject that you just can't say who's responsible," explained one woman. People go on to point out that every member of the community (not only parents) has a role to play when it comes to improving education. From an Atlanta man: "You can understand why people who don't have any children don't get involved, but they should be interested because these kids could be tomorrow's employees."[16]

People who focus on education rather than just schooling seem to be more in touch with their social, political, and economic objectives. That is what remarks like "education is important to everything" mean. Members of the research team all heard people say that education is a key to eliminating racism, strengthening the economy, safeguarding the environment, and so on. These goals touch a wide range of interests, making claims on almost everyone. As a woman from Baton Rouge reasoned, if we accepted the proposition that education is everyone's responsibility, "there would be a community strategy, not a school strategy, for educating every single child; everyone would have a role to play."[17]

Harnessing All That Educates

When we describe the many kinds of education a community needs, we implicate a host of community agencies. People interviewed in our research recognized that most of our institutions educate, from libraries and museums to television stations and computer centers. (Chattanooga has so many educating agencies that its citizens prepared a map showing where

---

16 The Harwood Group, *How Citizens View Education: Their Public Concerns and Private Actions* ([Dayton, Ohio]: Kettering Foundation, 1993), p. 11.

17 John Doble, memorandum to Damon Higgins and Randa Slim, 19 July 1993, Kettering Foundation, Dayton, Ohio, p. 4.

they are located.) Businesses, for instance, continue to teach in much the way craft guilds did centuries ago, through the apprentice system. Each institution also brings its own unique array of resources to bear on education. Kathleen Martin, of Texas Christian University, points out that teaching mathematics and science, in all their complexity, requires more resources than are found in schools; and she suggests that many other agencies can complement school instruction in these areas. A zoo's staff can teach from its unique perspective on evolution; a storage business has a special setting for teaching about space; a builder can teach out of a knowledge of materials.[18]

The education that is "out there" could enrich the education that goes on in schools, or so many of those interviewed thought. "What they're teaching kids nowadays is not what they will need to survive in this world" was a frequent observation, leading to suggestions like "Show them what the company does" or "Kids should get exposure to the jobs they might be doing."[19]

Using All Who Educate

Individuals as well as institutions can and, at some point, usually do educate. I am not referring only to middle-class Americans with college degrees; people from low-income neighborhoods who may not have finished high school often have a wide range of skills and experiences to share. According to evidence from the Solomon Project of the Hubert H. Humphrey Institute at the University of Minnesota, even those who have had little formal instruction know what makes for excellence in education.[20]

Our research reinforces this conclusion. From 1992 to 1994, the foundation tested a community workbook called *Take Charge* in several low-income neighborhoods. The workbook consists of a series of questions,

18 Kathleen Martin, telephone interview by Gina Paget, transcript, 22 June 1995, Kettering Foundation, Dayton, Ohio.

19 John Doble Research Associates, "Summaries of Five Research Projects," pp. 3–5.

20 Project Public Life, *Teaching Politics: 1991 Annual Report* (Minneapolis: Project Public Life, Hubert H. Humphrey Institute of Public Affairs, 1991).

such as: What do you know how to do well? Where did you learn it? What helped you learn it? Have you ever taught anyone anything? What do you think made your teaching effective? Participants in the discussions, though often likely to begin by saying, "I never taught anybody anything" (perhaps because they associated teaching with formal instruction in schools), went on to mention numerous ways in which they had educated. They had taught basic reading and mathematics, self-respect, and skills like cooking or sewing or taking care of equipment, as well as the virtues of patience, persistence, and sacrifice.

To be sure, the research team encountered feelings of hopelessness, a penchant for thinking of people as victims, and an uncertainty about abilities. Yet they also found untapped capacities and an appreciation of the value of education ("the best thing in the world"), along with a willingness to teach others. For example, a group of African-American parents who attend the same church was concerned that young people had too few learning opportunities. After working their way through the *Take Charge* sessions and holding an additional planning meeting, they decided to ensure that youngsters were exposed to something new and interesting at least once a month. They resolved to "take charge" of the children's education, reaffirming the importance of a kind of public education in their church's mission.

America could probably increase its capacity to educate many times over if it were possible to harness all its educational resources in ways that made them more complementary, more mutually reinforcing.

Step Three: Reconnecting the Public to Its Schools

People taking charge of education, everyone with a role to play — this should describe a public well connected to its schools through the community's commitment to education. So why aren't these connections evident all across America? Even in communities where education is considered very important and seen as everyone's responsibility, the schools and the public may be miles apart. The reason: there may be no agreement on the respective roles of citizens and educators.

"Reconnecting the public to its schools" will be a meaningless slogan unless we can clarify the division of responsibility between professional educators and the public. As former National Education Association President Mary Hatwood Futrell has pointed out, although many reform proposals call for increased collaboration with communities, "the question of who should do what is left unanswered."

I don't think we can expect that many people will join together to improve schools or that educators will welcome them to play a larger part in the effort unless we are clear about the particular roles a public — and only a public — can play.

Political Roles for the Public

Reestablishing a Public Mandate: Surely the first responsibilities of a democratic citizenry are to make decisions about public purposes, to figure out the educational means to carry out its purposes and, from those, to establish the broad mandates for schools that would, in effect, recharter them. Political roles for citizens can't be restricted to approving tax levies, electing school boards, and supporting special events ("bake some cookies to pay for the band trip"). Citizens have to be engaged in setting missions for schools within the context of public objectives.

While mandates for schools have to be based on the public's purposes, communities never settle on these all at once or in general terms. We decide our purposes issue by issue as we determine what to do about the environment, the economy, care of the ill and indigent, and the like. And we have to continue deciding them because the challenges a community faces continue to change. An objective appropriate for the 1960s may be out of date by the 1990s. So, when I say that citizens have to choose their purposes, I don't have in mind that everyone will go to city hall on a given morning and produce a declaration of public objectives to be framed and hung on the wall. The most important thing communities can do to meet their responsibility for defining purposes and giving mandates is to create "public space," where people can continue to hammer out their purposes through ongoing, deliberative dialogue.

Kettering research shows that some communities are rich in these opportunities for people to become involved, while others are relatively impoverished.[21] The difference makes a difference. Public space may be a monthly town meeting, forums organized by several civic and educational groups, or a series of neighborhood gatherings. In Grand Rapids, for example, more than 40 organizations hold public forums on 3 NIF issues each year, creating an information highway that is particularly civic. Where the meetings are and who arranges them aren't so important. What happens at them is critical. Citizens must have ample opportunities for serious, inclusive, face-to-face deliberation.

Public interests begin to emerge when citizens use these occasions to ask themselves such questions as: What in our community is most valuable to us? Why is it really important? People usually respond initially: a new community center, more police, better jobs, or the like. As they dig deeper and ask themselves *why* they want a new center, more police, or better jobs, they get to the things that are most valuable — perhaps a stronger sense of community, greater personal safety, or more financial security.[22]

Identifying what is deeply valuable to people sets the stage for the obvious next question: How do we get what we want? And responding to that question leads to discussions of education — all kinds of education — because, as people say again and again, "Education is important to everything." A community center, for example — a building — won't create a stronger sense of community. A center has to have programs, and many of those programs will be educational: seminars on local history, workshops on the environment, after-school projects for youngsters.

Although people are not in the habit of connecting educational practices with public purposes in this way, they can; in fact, they may even warm to the task. As one person said, after completing an exercise in identifying the

21 The Harwood Group, "Forming Public Capital: Observations from Two Communities" (Kettering Foundation, Dayton, Ohio, August 1995, photocopied).

22 The Harwood Group, "Hard Talk Discussion Group Report: Insights into How Citizens Talk about Education and Community" (Kettering Foundation, Dayton, Ohio, 1991, photocopied).

educational imperatives that grow out of community goals, "People don't normally link education and their community, [but] I think it is quite striking." Someone else added, "We need to talk about education and our community together, so that we can see what we really want out of education."[23]

When communities begin by looking at public purposes before proceeding to educational means, they create a context for thinking about mandates for schools, with the result that people know something about where schools fit into the larger scheme of things. It is not unlike buying a toy that needs to be assembled — we don't know the function of a particular part until we see a diagram of the finished product. What a school does makes little sense unless we know how its mission relates to the community's educational goals and public purposes.

Keeping an eye on the community context helps connect what would otherwise be technical debates over school policies with people's broader concerns. Without that context, as one citizen said, "there isn't much integration between schools and the community. They are very separate . . . and that is why people think about them separately." To some, that separation doesn't seem right. "Schools are really a subset of the larger community," a discussion group member observed; "you can't talk about one without talking about the other."[24]

Kettering found that one of the major benefits of public forums that began by focusing on the community rather than the schools was avoiding the usual "solution wars," which are ongoing disputes over specific proposals for reform.[25] When people begin by talking about the schools, factions tend to spring up on all sides and familiar proposals reemerge: teachers have their recommendations, taxpayers have their own ideas, business leaders have still others. Solution wars put citizens off. One person commented, "The different factions in this community no longer appear to be working for the common good; it's too much of 'I want this and she

23 Ibid., p. 6.

24 Ibid., p. 7.

25 Michele Archie, "Testing the 'Fresh Start/Hard Talk' Exercise" (Kettering Foundation, Dayton, Ohio, 2 April 1995, photocopied).

wants that.'"[26]

Champions of solutions maintain that everyone knows what the problem is; but, in fact, most people know only their own experience with a given problem. It is not uncommon for citizens to spend their energy debating which of a number of predetermined solutions is best, seemingly unaware that there is no agreement on the nature of the problem. Leaders have battled over various financing proposals, for example, when there was no community consensus that additional funds would make a real difference.

Starting community discussions around what is most valuable to people, with public concerns and aspirations, both lessens the likelihood of being trapped in solution wars and builds the foundation for a public mandate.

Judging Results: If the public has to decide what the school's mandate should be, surely citizens also have to determine whether that mandate is carried out, whether they are getting the results they want. That requires more than setting standards and holding schools accountable. Unfortunately, as I said earlier, our conventional ways of defining success and measuring results can (and often do) undermine the principal ingredient of success, namely, a strong sense of public responsibility.

Let me use a hypothetical illustration. A community might decide to improve its schools by having professionals set measurable standards of success. Local districts might have wide latitude in implementing the standards, but the outcomes would be calculated against these preestablished criteria, in much the same way a carpenter measures a board. The community would be limited to determining success according to standards it hadn't set. That inevitably undercuts the public's sense of accountability, of citizens holding themselves, not just schools, responsible for outcomes.

A further limitation is that measuring success in the way carpenters measure boards confines us to evaluating only those results that are quantifiable — and many of the outcomes we want are not. Even more

26 The Harwood Group, "Hard Talk Discussion Group Report," p. 15.

serious, before we can measure our success, we have to decide what success means; and that decision is an inescapable public responsibility. Not only does a community have the right to specify the results it wants, making that determination is a critical aspect of community learning. The real purpose of assessing what happens isn't to lay blame but to discover what must be done next. In the process of comparing what we intended with what happened (where measuring can be useful), we learn a great deal about how we function as a community. We may even change our definition of success after seeing the results of our work.

Public accountability requires a public mechanism for direct examination. Tennessee's "community report card" system of the 1980s had elements of this kind of process. Under this arrangement, groups of citizens set school standards within the context of community purposes. State legislation funded these community groups for five years, and some of them are still in business.[27]

Protecting the Larger Public Interests/Convening Disparate Factions: Another important role for the public is to be a bulwark in times of crisis, protecting schools from special interests. Without a supportive public, with interconnected purposes and a common sense of direction, schools are helpless before the besieging forces of these interests. Public organizations, broad based, inclusive, and focused on the community as a whole rather than on a single issue or cause, are needed to mediate between the larger public interests (which James Madison called "permanent and enduring interests") and the interests of particular groups (which Madison called "factions"). Special interests are not inappropriate, but they have to be reconciled with the interests of the larger public. Only citizens — with other citizens — can do that.

Are there public organizations that can play this role? Certainly there have been in the not too distant past. Citizen alliances played a decisive political role in rallying round schools during the desegregation struggles of

27 Jennie Vanetta Carter Thomas, telephone interview by Kathy Whyde Jesse, transcript, May 1995, Kettering Foundation, Dayton, Ohio.

the 1960s and 1970s. Voluntary organizations sprang up from Dallas to Pontiac, Michigan, and the courts used these citizen committees in conjunction with their rulings.[28] We might do well to recapture that experience. I wonder why citizen alliances like those that rallied communities to face a crisis in the 1970s are not being used as the schools face new crises over drugs, violence, and moral issues in the 1990s.

Of course, special interests sometimes have the upper hand. Combatants may not be willing to abandon their particular commitments in favor of some abstract common good; however, it may not even be necessary for them to do that. Acknowledging these interests, which isn't the same as endorsing them, can move people away from conflict and pave the way to finding connections and overlapping concerns among citizens whose priorities differ.[29]

In the case of the committees that responded to desegregation orders, the members certainly had conflicting interests. Some favored complete and immediate integration of the schools; others, who did not necessarily favor integration (particularly if it involved busing), were more concerned with preventing racial strife from enveloping their communities. I recall a civic leader from Texas who didn't like busing, but he did like his community and didn't want to see it divided, as others had been. Each faction depended on the other, recognizing that integration was not going to proceed quickly or smoothly in the face of implacable opposition and that community stability was unlikely to be maintained without the cooperation of those advocating change. Despite their differences, the groups had connected or interdependent interests; they could work together on school desegregation *and* community stability.

Unhappily, this kind of interdependence isn't always self-evident — we have to discover it. And that is where public organizations have been useful, bringing conflicting parties together, not to negotiate a settlement of their

28 Elinor Hart, *Desegregation without Turmoil: The Role of the Multi-Racial Community Coalition in Preparing for Smooth Transition* ([New York]: National Conference of Christians and Jews, 1977).

29 David A. Lax and James K. Sebenius, "Interests: The Measure of Negotiation," in *Negotiation Theory and Practice,* edited by J. William Breslin and Jeffrey Z. Rubin (Cambridge, Mass.: Program on Negotiation at Harvard Law School, 1991), p. 161.

differences, but to broaden their outlooks and find intersecting interests.

Reflecting on a career of involvement in this kind of activity, Ernesto Cortes, of the Industrial Areas Foundation, explained, "You begin to see your interests as broadening in relationships with other people, particularly as you begin to have serious conversations and you begin to identify with other people's experiences."[30] Cortes' point is that our perceptions of what is in our interest aren't static. We can mature politically just as we can mature intellectually and socially. Joan Martin-Brown, associate regional director for North America of the United Nations Environment Program, recalls how her global interests evolved from a very parochial preoccupation. Initially limited to a concern about her hometown environment, that concern broadened to include the environment of her state and country and, eventually, the planet. Perhaps this evolution was driven by an expanding sense of what matters over time, culminating in a recognition of what biologists call long-term self-interests.

For citizens to play a role in finding connected and interdependent interests in the typical community, which is filled with special interests, they may need a particular type of civic organization, one committed to being a "boundary spanner." You can find a good example of this kind of association by looking up Dorothy Stuck and her colleagues in Arkansas. Stuck has published local newspapers, worked for the federal government, and now runs what she insists on calling a "resultancy" (rather than a consultancy) with her friend Nan Snow. In 1982, Dorothy Stuck and a group of people she had met over the years established the Wilowe Institute, an organization in which citizens could address important policy matters facing their state. Unlike the typical blue-ribbon commission or coalition, the institute was built around an ongoing, statewide forum, and its members represented no one except themselves. Its aim was simple: to connect different people and disparate interests throughout Arkansas, so they could tackle common problems. Evidently the strategy worked — Wilowe has had a rich history as a catalyst for a host of cooperative efforts.

---

30 Ernesto Cortes, Jr., "On Leadership: Interview with Ernesto Cortes, Jr.," interview by Noëlle McAfee, transcript, 19 and 22 November 1992, Kettering Foundation, Dayton, Ohio, p. 24.

Overcoming Institutional Barriers: Boundary-spanning organizations can also help citizens bring about changes in school bureaucracies, not by opposing the system, but by modeling different ways of working.

Structure, routines, and bureaucratic procedures in schools can make change impossible, even when educators genuinely want it. John Goodlad pointed out in 1984 that the power relationships controlling the behavior of systems defeat reforms.[31] This happens, Seymour Sarason observed, "not because there is a grand conspiracy or because of mulish stubbornness in resisting change or because educators are uniquely unimaginative or uncreative (which they are not) but rather because recognizing and trying to change power relationships, especially in complicated, traditional institutions, is among the most complex tasks human beings can undertake."[32]

More recently, David Conley arrived at the same conclusion. Recognizing that schools began as extensions of their communities, he found that they have become increasingly bureaucratic and separated from them: "While bureaucratic structures serve to protect schools from arbitrary and capricious interventions in their functioning, they also lessen the ability of schools to adapt and change."[33]

Despite these obstacles, boundary-spanning organizations can stimulate change by bringing different community institutions together to experiment with new ways of working together. These experiments can sometimes reach deep inside the bureaucracies of the institutions involved.

Too often, educators talk primarily to educators, business leaders to business leaders, police to police. By bringing all sectors of the community and all kinds of people to the same table, citizens' organizations have been effective in modifying working relationships among institutions. You might say that they have built civic versions of Noah's ark to reassemble their

---

31 John I. Goodlad, *A Place Called School: Prospects for the Future* (New York: McGraw-Hill Book Company, 1984).

32 Seymour Sarason, *The Predictable Failure of Educational Reform* (San Francisco: Jossey-Bass, 1990), pp. 6–7.

33 David T. Conley, *Roadmap to Restructuring: Policies, Practices, and the Emerging Visions of Schooling* (Eugene: ERIC Clearinghouse on Educational Management, University of Oregon, 1993), p. 311.

communities. The members, who work in the square boxes of hierarchical order, are typically seated in a circle; and the arrangement of chairs both encourages and reflects a restructuring of their relationships. Talking to one another from different perspectives prompts new insights — new ways of seeing problems and new ways of seeing each other. These insights remain with institutional leaders after they leave the meetings and influence the way they behave outside the civic organizations. This can result in new partnerships, such as those that pair schools with other educating agencies. These partnerships can, in turn, affect attitudes within the members' institutions.[34] And, as institutions change their perceptions of each other, they may change their operating procedures as well.

Boundary-spanning organizations can have this effect because, not being subject to bureaucratic constraints, they can become laboratories that allow institutional leaders to test new ways of working together, which is usually impossible in formal settings. Informality prompts a degree of candor and freedom to experiment that official meetings discourage. Without the kind of laboratories citizens can provide, experimentation occurs only behind closed doors and involves only a few people, if it happens at all. The laboratories can synthesize diverse initiatives and work out comprehensive approaches to problems that use the full range of a community's resources; through them, citizens contribute an entirely new array of problem-solving options.

Citizens can influence what goes on inside school bureaucracies through the capacity of their boundary-spanning organizations to bring schools back into the community. We all know that any group tends to resist external demands, and yet boundary spanners can neutralize much of the resistance by having teachers and administrators at the table with other citizens. If the changes proposed by these meetings are communitywide and not directed solely at one group or one institution, they are more likely to be acceptable.

---

34 John M. Bryson et al., *Leadership for the Common Good: Tackling Public Problems in a Shared-Power World* (San Francisco: Jossey-Bass, 1992).

These changes can reach into the very heart of school systems — to their missions. As inclusive civic organizations reassess a community's problems, they take the first step in reassessing those missions. School bureaucracies, like all other bureaucracies, derive their functions from a given set of circumstances and concerns. They need influence from outside if they are to reshape them to accommodate changes in those circumstances and concerns.[35]

Educational Roles for the Public

The public's role is not limited to politics; the public also has to educate, has to be one of the authors of the schooling it wants. In fact, it may be essential for citizens to be directly involved in educating if they are to fulfill their political roles. Why? If we think of education as part of our work as citizens, it changes our relationship to schools, making it more likely that we will see them as our agents, as institutions that help us carry out our responsibilities. And schools that are doing *our* job have a greater claim on our political allegiance.

Citizens can educate in at least three ways through a community:

By Motivating: Broad public support for schools apparently encourages students to work harder. In Tennessee, test scores improved even before legislated reforms were put in place.[36] How could that have happened? Political campaigns preceding the legislation evidently sent a powerful message to both teachers and students: people thought what teachers did was important and cared whether or not students learned. Because it is widely recognized that learning is affected by the amount of social support young people receive,[37] the rise in test scores probably shouldn't have been surprising.

---

35 Ibid.

36 Jennie Vanetta Carter Thomas, "How Three Governors Involved the Public in Passing Their Education Reform Programs" (Ed.D. dissertation, George Peabody College for Teachers at Vanderbilt University, 1992), pp. 35–36.

37 James S. Coleman and Thomas Hoffer found that the motivating power of individual adults who were connected socially and able to establish common expectations regarding the behavior of young people is greater than that of adults who are not socially linked. See Coleman and Hoffer, *Public and Private High Schools: The Impact of Communities* (New York: Basic Books, 1987), pp. 221-233.

The public can do more than cheer from the sidelines. Citizens have provided motivation by getting into the game themselves, becoming directly involved in teaching through community institutions. That has created social norms that make education everyone's responsibility, not just the job of teachers, administrators, and parents. These norms are evident in comments to the effect that "everybody is trying to teach the kids." At one point in Atlanta's history, following a concerted effort to enlist citizens, businesses began to sponsor magnet schools, while churches and synagogues ran tutorial programs. The community was teaching its young people by using *all* its educational resources.[38] Communities that consciously try to educate *as communities* may educate best.

By Providing a Context for Learning: The public or community can also provide a valuable context for learning. Context helps students understand *why* they should learn what they are being taught. Context gives learning the purpose and meaning that make it real. In Jackson County, Kentucky, for example, where quilting is a familiar community activity, the K–3 Mathematics Project used quilts to teach basic geometric concepts. Cutting shapes out of construction paper to make patterns for quilt patches made the concepts of "triangle" and "pentangle" concrete, understandable, and significant.[39]

Citizens seem to appreciate the community's potential to provide a context for learning. At a town meeting in Baton Rouge, one woman put it this way:

> I believe that schools should be teaching math and that [students] should go to these places [in the community] to practice the concepts you learn in school or to see how they are applied. In a library, you practice the skills you learned about research and referencing, in a museum you see a mummy which you learned about in school. Kids

---

38 Alonzo A. Crim, "A Community of Believers Creates a Community of Achievers," *Educational Record* (special double issue) 68/69 (fall 1987/winter 1988): 45.

39 Susan Ohanian, *Garbage Pizza, Patchwork Quilts, and Math Magic* (New York: W. H. Freeman, 1992), pp. 184–186.

should go to Exxon and see on-the-job application of the trigonometry they've learned.[40]

Robert Moses, a civil rights activist in Mississippi during the 1960s and the recipient of a MacArthur Foundation "genius" grant, has captured this woman's vision in his Algebra Project, which demonstrates effective use of a community to provide context. The project began in Boston after Moses became unhappy with the instruction his eldest daughter was receiving in her eighth grade mathematics class. Before Moses introduced the project, few students at his daughter's school took the advanced-placement qualifying exam in mathematics, and few of those who did were able to pass it. After ten years with the program in place, the school's graduates ranked second in advanced-placement test scores.

Believing that difficult mathematical concepts like negative numbers could be more readily explained to students if they were linked to everyday applications, Moses looked for a vivid example. The familiar Red Line subway route provided the context he needed:

> Herding his students into a subway car, Moses took them inbound to Boston, then back past Central Square to the end of the line in Cambridge. Back in class, armed with magic markers, students assigned a value of zero to the Central Square station. Soon they had transformed the train route into a number line with positive values for inbound stops, negatives for outbound. Students got the point, a fun ride and a chance to make art out of numbers. One boy who used to hide behind a piano during math class emerged. Groans diminished. Resistance ebbed. Soon Moses was experimenting with other ways to teach algebraic concepts: zodiac games to teach multiplication and division and lemonade concentrate to teach ratios.[41]

---

40 Doble, memorandum to Higgins and Slim, p. 4.

41 Alexis Jetter, "Mississippi Learning," *New York Times*, 21 February 1993, sec. 6, p. 28.

By Making Available a Repository of Substantive Knowledge: Schools are marvelous repositories of substantive knowledge: mathematics, history, English literature. A community, on the other hand, is assumed not to have substantive knowledge — only knowledge of how to get along in the world. That just isn't so. While no other community institution proposes to replace the school, many of them teach the same subjects that are taught in classrooms: natural history museums offer courses in ecology, art museums teach art history and train artists.[42]

On the basis of articles in the newspapers of seven cities around the country, Kettering researchers found a broad spectrum of community organizations teaching school subjects. These educating institutions included eight science museums, four history museums, three art museums, seven theaters, two choirs, two orchestras, and four libraries. Thirteen other institutions, including the Latin American Day Center in Charlotte; the YMCA in Willimantic, Connecticut; the North Carolina Zoological Park; and the Trailside Nature Center in Cincinnati, also reported offering substantive classes. In all, over 40 teaching organizations were identified, with courses ranging from "The Ice Age" to "Egyptian Textiles" to "The Planetary System."[43]

Although the subjects are often the same, out-of-school instruction differs significantly from classroom teaching. Lauren Resnick has pointed out that schools focus primarily on individual learners, while other educating institutions in the community teach people to learn together as part of learning to work together. Schools encourage symbolic and abstract thinking, while instruction outside the school is likely to be more concrete and practical.[44]

---

42 It is instructive to note that home schools often use the resources of the community to provide education in subjects like music and environmental sciences (*Morning Edition,* National Public Radio, 24 October 1995).

43 Kathy Whyde Jesse, "Newspaper Study" (Kettering Foundation, Dayton, Ohio, 1994, photocopied).

44 Lauren B. Resnick, "The 1987 Presidential Address: Learning in School and Out," *Educational Researcher* 16 (December 1987): 13–20.

Educators and Citizens: Do Their Roles Conflict?

To say that the community educates doesn't diminish the importance of schools. The rationale for maintaining public schools isn't that they are a sole source — that is the rationale of witch doctors.

The proposition that the community has to take responsibility for education in order for its schools to teach most effectively shouldn't threaten educators. In fact, teachers understand the principle behind this proposition with respect to the role of parents. They often say that, unless parents take responsibility for the education of their children, it is very difficult for teachers to be effective in the classroom. In a sense, the public or community is simply the parent writ large. The principle is no different.

Educators are rightly proud of being professional, which implies holding themselves accountable to their own standards of good teaching and effective administration. Professionals, however, particularly those who deal directly with the public, have become increasingly aware of how much their effectiveness depends on citizens assuming their share of responsibility.

Ronald Heifetz, a physician now teaching government at Harvard University, has a particularly apt way of explaining the inability of professionals to do their jobs without assistance from the public. Heifetz knows from his background in medicine that problems differ significantly from one another and that there are corresponding differences in the remedies they require. Medical problems range from routine conditions that can be cured by a physician to more serious ones, for which there is no clear-cut diagnosis and no technical fix. Think of the difference between a broken arm and advanced diabetes; the remedy for the former is a straightforward one, not so for the latter. With the most serious problems, the patient and physician have to combine forces. Similarly, our most serious problems in education are those whose very definitions are unclear and whose remedies are undetermined. These are problems that professionals can't solve by themselves. Without the commitment of an engaged public, they have little hope of being successful.[45]

45 Ronald Heifetz, *Leadership without Easy Answers* (Cambridge, Mass.: Harvard University Press, Belknap Press, 1994), pp. 69–76.

CHAPTER 4

PUBLIC LIFE AND SCHOOLS

Another Way to Think about
the Relationship

Will public-building strategies work over the long haul? Is there any correlation between the public life of a community and the quality of its public schools? I believe there is.[1] Robert Putnam, professor of government at Harvard University, has shown that an effective government and a prosperous economy in north central Italy are associated with a healthy public life. His study suggests that a healthy public life may also be positively correlated with good public schools.[2]

What is a healthy public life? That is the subject of this chapter, which introduces another way of thinking about the public or community. It calls for a paradigm shift of the kind Thomas Kuhn found so useful in

---

1   It is interesting to note that colonial Dorchester, which created a rich public life through town meetings, established the first public or free schools in the colonies a few years after the town meetings began. See Maude Pinney Kuhns, *The "Mary and John": A Story of the Founding of Dorchester, Massachusetts, 1630* (Rutland, Vt.: Charles E. Tuttle Co., 1943).

2   Robert D. Putnam, *Making Democracy Work: Civic Traditions in Modern Italy* (Princeton, N.J.: Princeton University Press, 1993).

understanding breakthroughs in the evolution of scientific thought. Conventional paradigms, or ways of seeing and approaching problems, can obscure important characteristics of those problems and so misdirect our efforts to solve them. The paradigm that controls the way we approach the problems of schools seems to prevent our seeing elements of what Ronald Heifetz has labeled a "Type III" situation, one that professional skills and resources alone can't remedy.

The analytical frameworks of scholars like Robert Putnam, Vaughn Grisham, and Douglass North give us a new paradigm for understanding societies, communities, and the public. They invite attention to what some call the "soft side" of the social order, such as processes for problem solving and types of civic associations, which may have everything to do with whether people become public citizens, whether towns and cities develop a sense of community. Because typical discussions of the public or community don't deal with factors like "civil infrastructure" or processes like "public deliberation" and "civic learning," it is a bit of a leap to connect them to what is happening in our schools. Yet that is precisely what the research on public life and civil society encourages us to do — to rethink the meaning of public engagement and community involvement in light of what this research suggests about the way publics and communities are constituted.

According to Putnam, a healthy public life, or strong civil society, consists of networks of civic associations, norms of reciprocity, and social trust that result in high levels of voluntary cooperation. People are involved in public matters and in relationships that run horizontally (among equals) instead of vertically (between haves and have-nots). While Putnam found these characteristics in some areas, they were noticeably absent in others. People in the "uncivil" areas didn't participate in either local politics or social organizations, and their relationships tended to be hierarchical, with the have-nots very dependent on the wealthy.

Similar studies, which have looked at the quality of public life in the United States, have found communities with many of the characteristics of the towns in north central Italy. Tupelo, Mississippi, where Elvis Presley was born, is often cited as an example.[3] At one time, it was called the poorest town in the poorest county in the poorest state of the union — a community unlikely ever to have a healthy public life. Small (its population is about 30,000) and located in a rural area, Tupelo has no special advantages: no large body of water, no nearby metropolitan center, and no government installation with a large federal budget. Until 1980, there wasn't even a four-lane highway within 75 miles. Today, its per capita income is close to that of Atlanta, and its prosperity extends into the surrounding area. In each of the past 12 years, Lee County has added over a thousand new industrial jobs and even more service jobs.

A large proportion of the people have a strong sense of community as well as a willingness to take responsibility; the public "owns" the town's major civic projects. Tupelo has a rich array of organizations and networks, which provide opportunities for citizens to define and redefine their problems and make decisions about how to act. Of course, this is not a perfect community. The local development foundation has been compared to the political "bosses" who ran local governments at the turn of the century. Some prominent citizens don't believe in public participation and think decisions should be in the hands of a small elite. Most, however, are convinced that the upper tier of leadership has to create even stronger ties to rank-and-file citizens because, as the town grows, new people and new problems create new challenges. On the whole, Tupelo is a community with a flourishing civic life, which has been able to reproduce itself decade after decade.

What about the public schools? Those in Tupelo have been consistently rated among the best in the region, and the Educational Leadership Foundation has designated the school system one of five national centers to receive funds for innovative programs. The community and the schools

---

3 See Vaughn L. Grisham's book, tentatively titled *It Can Be Done: The Tupelo Model* (Washington, D.C.: Rural Economic Policy Program, Aspen Institute, in press). For a study of communities other than Tupelo, see Heartland Center for Leadership Development, *Clues to Rural Community Survival,* 8th ed. (Lincoln, Nebr.: Heartland Center for Leadership Development, 1992). See also Otis White, "The Best-Run Town in Florida," *Florida Trend* 17 (February 1995): 36–43, a discussion of Delray Beach.

have an excellent relationship and communicate through a variety of channels.[4]

You might ask whether the strong economy isn't the reason for this community's healthy public life. Obviously, each reinforces the other. But, when Putnam investigated a similar question in his study of Italian towns, he found that it was public life rather than the economy that made the difference, that north central Italy was not civil because it was rich but rich because it was civil. The people of Tupelo agree. They say their prosperous economy has been the result of community development; their economic strategies have been essentially public-building strategies.

While studies like those of Tupelo and the towns of north central Italy don't prove that a healthy public life leads to good schools, they do suggest that there is a correlation, that public-building strategies could, over the long term, effect educational improvement. In other words, there is reason to think that public life and schools are related in vital ways, reason to try to understand the dynamics of the relationship, reason to find out what public-building strategies could accomplish.

The obvious next question is whether it is possible to improve schools through a deliberate effort to strengthen public life. Although we won't know until some communities try, there are already experiments with public-building strategies that point the way, even though they don't focus specifically on schools. One city, Chicago, is strengthening the public sector as a strategy to revitalize its social service system. The Chicago Community Trust, one leader in this venture, thinks of social service improvement as a matter of community development. The trust has worked out a civil-investment strategy to restore the informal social services that contribute to civic vitality. Citizens, not agency administrators, are the prime actors. They are doing the things that only citizens can do — simple but essential things, like organizing more baseball teams. The trust is buying baseball gloves rather than hours of therapy. The idea isn't to bypass the service

---

4 Grisham, *It Can Be Done,* chap. 1.

agencies but to complement their work with neighborhood programs as part of restructuring their relationship with the community.[5]

Critical to the new strategies is a thorough knowledge of the structures and processes essential to a well-functioning public sector. The next part of this chapter describes how a healthy public life is constructed.

Checking on the Health of Public Life

Research on towns like Tupelo helps identify the elements of a healthy public life and gives us standards for assessing the health of our own communities. These studies suggest that we look at (1) civil infrastructure, including types of citizens' organizations and their communication networks; (2) particular processes like civic learning and public decision making; (3) the nature of the leadership; (4) the mind-set that informs civic action; (5) the relationship of citizens to institutions; and (6) such intangibles as sense of community and norms of cooperation. Checking up on public life may be a good way to start the process of strengthening it.[6]

Looking at Civil Infrastructure and Channels of Communication

A public needs regular opportunities, occasions, meetings, or "space," to do its work; it also needs open channels of communication that are linked in crosscutting networks. Communities have to have places where different people can talk about common problems — either formally, in town meetings or forums, or informally, in one-to-one or small-group conversations. These places are essential for generating political will, solving public problems and, most of all, creating citizens. So, one of the first things to check is how much public space a community has. The sum total of public space, along with the way it is ordered and connected, might be called a community's civil infrastructure.

One of the distinctive features of a community with a healthy public life

---

5   Marvin R. Cohen, "An Exercise in Civility: A 'Project Eighty' Report" (Chicago Community Trust, June 1995, photocopied), pp. 22–23.

6   The Kettering Foundation has a workbook called *Community Checkup,* which communities have been using to assess the quality of their public life.

is the amount of effort that goes into building this infrastructure. On the "ground floor," numerous ad hoc associations (small groups like local development councils and neighborhood alliances) provide points of entry, where people can begin to get "involved." More inclusive and more broadly focused civic clubs and facilitating organizations (community foundations, for instance) are on the next level. Overarching everything, umbrella organizations, or "boundary spanners," provide connections that hold it all together. All the associations function as channels of communication, so the civil infrastructure is also a communications infrastructure.

Civil infrastructure rests on an informal social system. Festivals, Little League baseball games, soccer matches, neighborhood parties, and potluck dinners bring people together.[7] More than social events, these gatherings help people form closer ties to their communities. They chat before and after church services; they talk at weddings and festivals; they sound off at bars and bingo parlors. Many of their conversations are about issues of the day, common social and economic problems, and deep political concerns. Ray Oldenburg has called the sites for these conversations the "great good places" of a community. They are remarkably similar to good homes in the comfort and support they offer.[8]

In order for social gatherings to strengthen public life, however, some have to have particular characteristics — they have to build public capital rather than purely social capital.[9] There have to be occasions where people can get to know one another as individuals; it's not enough for community members to "know" each other simply on the basis of social status or family background. Also, people must have opportunities to engage in a larger conversation about the well-being of the community as a whole. And there

---

7   The Harwood Group, "Forming Public Capital: Observations from Two Communities," (Kettering Foundation, Dayton, Ohio, August 1995, photocopied), p. 3.

8   Ray Oldenburg, *The Great Good Place: Cafés, Coffee Shops, Community Centers, Beauty Parlors, General Stores, Bars, Hangouts and How They Get You through the Day* (New York: Paragon House, 1989), p. 42.

9   Here, the term "social capital" refers to bonds of loyalty and trust among family and friends, which can be drawn on like capital in a bank when someone needs help. Social capital, or the lack of it, affects public life. "Public capital," on the other hand, grows out of the associations, civic networks, and ways of relating that join people who are essentially strangers in the act of community problem solving.

have to be inclusive gatherings, inclusive with respect to who organizes them as well as who takes part in them.[10] Citizens must be able to find others who have similar or related interests.

Public life itself takes full shape where people join not just with friends, neighbors, and coworkers but with the relative strangers of the larger community. These meetings often occur in the kinds of ad hoc associations Alexis de Tocqueville found in the nineteenth century and that still flourish today. The public forums of Grand Rapids and Kalamazoo are good examples. In Grand Rapids, 30 to 40 civic and educational organizations convene the community to deal with 3 major issues each year, using the National Issues Forums books. They have been doing this for nearly 15 years. These meetings aren't just social events; people deliberate over difficult choices on tough issues. They give their own names to their problems and sort out the possibilities for change. As they struggle over making difficult decisions together, they make connections and build relationships, not only for fellowship, but for acting together.

The next tier of associations consists of formal civic clubs, leagues, and nongovernmental organizations, which usually have offices with signs on the doors, staffs, and budgets. Some, like the Wilowe Institute, function as umbrella or boundary-spanning organizations, encouraging communitywide discussions, developing a sense of interrelatedness, building networks, and promoting resource sharing.

Among the more interesting new civic structures are 22 Public Policy Institutes sponsored by universities like the University of California at Davis and associations like the National Council for the Social Studies. The summer institute at Pembroke State University in Robeson County, North Carolina, created to promote civic learning, is a good example.

Robeson County is made up of equal proportions of whites, African-Americans, and Native Americans, who have lived with poverty, segregation, and rural isolation for a long time. Eager to get people working together, Joe Oxendine, the first Lumbee Indian to become president of Pembroke State, and his assistant, Terry Hutchins, established the summer

10   The Harwood Group, "Forming Public Capital," p. 3.

institute to teach people the skills of making the choices that have to precede working cooperatively. The institute has been in business since 1992 and enrolls more than 200 civic leaders each summer, most of whom live in the area. Students like senior Tony Spalding have participated and remember the experience as an education in which people from all walks of life learned how to make tough decisions together, even though they had very different perspectives on the issues confronting them.

While educators can't create public space on their own, they need to pitch in as citizens and do their share of the work. In fact, that is already happening: a good many of the people who organize forums, create umbrella organizations, and teach in Public Policy Institutes are employees of public schools. Their public-building efforts could be the essential activities that establish a foundation for healthy public schools.

Checking Up on Critical Processes

While ad hoc associations, boundary-spanning organizations, and centers for civic learning are necessary structures, public life itself is made up of relationships, interactions, and exchanges; it is carried on through a particular kind of discourse, one that is highly deliberative. In checking the health of a community's public life, it is important to look at the public decision-making process to see how public it really is and whether the talk is conducive to working through tough choices.

Public decisions should be made intentionally and not by default. A good question to ask in a checkup is whether citizens are in the habit of making choices together and what that habit is.[11] Under the best circumstances, decision making starts modestly, moves slowly, and is not forced on the community. If citizens are going to be effective in dealing with their problems, they need ample opportunities to think about issues and work through their options, in both formal and informal settings. And community leaders have to tap into these settings if their initiatives are to succeed. Their conversations with citizens have to go both ways; they can't show up just to promote their own solutions. We have found that, in

11 David Mathews, *Community Politics,* rev. ed. (Dayton, Ohio: Kettering Foundation, [1995]), p. 30.

communities that have difficulty bringing people together, decisions tend to be forced on citizens — who usually respond with resistance, skepticism, and little support.[12]

It goes without saying that findings like these are important for strategies of public engagement or community involvement. We have concluded that public decision making must be preceded by what we are calling "civic learning," which is what we learn from and through our exchanges with one another. Civic learning allows us to know those things that we come to know only by talking together and never alone — what is valuable to us as a community, what our shared or interrelated interests are, whether we have compatible purposes, what we think we ought to do in responding to a problem. We don't discover those things as much as we create them; they don't preexist our talking together in the kind of talk that we use to teach ourselves before we act.[13]

Too often, leaders take months to study issues and make decisions among themselves yet allow the public little opportunity to learn. The usual practice is to promote a proposal of the leadership group with a collection of supporting facts intended to convince the public of its merits. Leaders put their energies into doing "a real selling job." Civic learning, however, is more than hearing proposals and amassing facts. People have to understand the perceptions that others bring to problems. None of us has exactly the same experience with any given issue, and our differing experiences lead to differing perceptions and differing ways of weighing what is most valuable. The new road that gets us across town more quickly may block someone else's access to neighbors. In order to know how we, as a community, see a problem like improving transportation, we have to synthesize a number of quite different perceptions. We can't really know what we think about an issue until we have talked about it. In other words,

12 The Harwood Group, "Forming Public Capital," p. 7. This study began with in-depth telephone interviews with "civic leaders" (e.g., officeholders, business executives) and "connective leaders" (i.e., people involved with a broad range of organizations and interests). Later, researchers interviewed rank-and-file citizens.

13 The concept of a kind of public talk that has didactic power is found in "Pericles' Funeral Oration," in Thucydides, *History of the Peloponnesian War*, bk. 2, sec. 40.

there are certain things we can't know alone but only through learning together. We have to construct a shared sense of what is happening, of the meaning of events in our lives. This kind of learning allows citizens to rename issues in public terms.

Civic learning is indispensable to public-forming; it is the self-starter for the kind of community development that citizens "own." Community building is essentially a matter of accelerating this learning. And keeping civic learning going year after year depends on a process for judging outcomes that is tied to learning together. I have already explained how the usual way of measuring results interferes with civic learning. Communities with a healthy public life are, above all, learning communities.

Reappraising Leadership

Surely a checkup of the quality of public life has to examine the leadership of a community. That requires more than the customary practice of evaluating the visible leaders, or key actors. Both weak communities and those with vibrant public sectors usually have able leaders. In fact, where public life is limited, there may be a small group of quite exceptional leaders. What is distinctive in communities with vigorous publics is not so much the qualifications of the leaders as their number, where they are located and, most of all, the way they interact with others. Forget any idea that strong publics don't have strong leaders. The fact is that they do. Nothing happens spontaneously; some courageous souls always have to step out first. Leaders, however, can be as strong in building a vibrant public sector as they are in demonstrating personal courage.

Where public life is vigorous, communities are "leaderful," with everyone expected to provide some measure of initiative.[14] Leaders function not as gatekeepers but as door openers, bent on widening participation. They also insist that others take ownership. Vaughn Grisham, who has studied Tupelo for 20 years, quotes one of its leaders, who was fond of

---

14 The Harwood Group, "Forming Public Capital," p. 5.

saying, "If you want a better community, you will have to do the work yourself."[15]

Watching what I will call "public leaders," observers are struck by how different their activities are from those of leaders in communities where public life is sickly. There, leaders are preoccupied with protecting turf or status and maintaining strict control over who is permitted to act and which actions are allowed. Leaders of robust communities, in sharp contrast, are busy marshaling resources for change; they are architects of new civil structures, bridge builders who link people with institutions and one sector of the community with another. They have a comprehensive outlook and a long time frame, which keep them from rushing to action in order to defuse one crisis after another. They have been described as crosscutting, or generalized, because they are concerned with the community as a whole and keep their focus on the larger picture. Open to learning from their failures, they are doggedly persistent without being stubborn.[16]

With so many providing leadership, "public leaders" are not clearly distinguishable from other citizens. There is no leadership class set apart from followers; "public leaders" are well integrated into their communities. Consequently, they have considerable latitude to do their jobs. For example, not every meeting has to be official. There are opportunities to gather for informal, off-the-record discussions, where comments are recorded without attribution. While the gist of what happens at these meetings may be reported, the accounts concentrate on issues rather than personalities.[17]

A number of "public leaders" come from positions of authority in businesses and other community institutions. Where public life is healthy, those in positions of authority see time spent in community building as directly beneficial to their bottom lines. Major institutions function as catalysts, helping to marshal resources for change (which aren't just dollars)

15 Grisham, *It Can Be Done,* chap. 3.
16 Ibid.
17 The Harwood Group, "Forming Public Capital," p. 4.

and encouraging the civic efforts of others. Just as important, they are careful never to become the driving forces.[18] This caution is especially important for schools that want to encourage community building. They have to operate in a way that stimulates public life while ensuring that educators never become "the leaders."

Where public life is minimal, institutions like schools and governments serve as a battleground on which a fragmented community fights over narrow interests. The institutions further weaken the community by failing to tap all of its strengths and resources.

Examining Mind-set

I wish I knew a better term to describe what is probably the most telling feature of public life because it would be easier to check. The best I can come up with is to say it is the pictures people carry in their heads about how problems are solved and "things get done." I would call these mind-sets or paradigms. Where public life flourishes, the mind-set is strikingly different from the perspective that informs politics-as-usual.[19] It promotes a more public form of politics, which is unlike typical civic activism in objectives, methods, and organization. People work as hard on improving the processes they use as they do on the outcomes they want. They don't divorce processes from products. Also, the scope of public projects is broad, reflecting a concern with the community as a whole. Our impression at Kettering is that these efforts aren't the typical categorical projects focusing on a single group of citizens or a single set of issues. Rather, the underlying objective seems to be to connect people and issues in more comprehensive pursuits.

Grisham calls these precepts "guiding principles." In Tupelo, they include such injunctions as "Never turn the work over to agencies that don't involve citizens." Widespread, inclusive participation, a prerequisite for public action, is an absolute maxim. Some of the guidelines are

---

18 Ibid.

19 I reported on these unique perspectives in greater detail in *Politics for People: Finding a Responsible Public Voice* (Urbana: University of Illinois Press, 1994), chaps. 8, 9.

commonsensical: "Build teams and use a team approach." Others are counterintuitive: "See everyone as a resource."[20]

John McKnight, a student of community organization, has made a career of explaining why this last principle — seeing people as assets rather than only as needs — is so critical. He insists that communities be viewed as the sum of the personal capacities of their citizens.[21] His directive could be extremely powerful in strengthening public life: when communities concentrate on capacities, they are likely to be more aware of the possibilities for action.

Anyone who lives in a community impoverished by a weak economy, or who sees people ill, homeless, and burdened by problems not of their own making, knows that individuals have needs. It's not surprising that one of the standard tools in conventional politics is "needs assessment." Emphasizing needs, however, tends to have unfortunate political side effects. People lose a sense of their capacities. So McKnight has created "capacity inventories," which help identify untapped personal talents and underused community resources. Every person can be seen as a glass half empty or half full, McKnight says. By labeling people with the names of their deficiencies (i.e., their needs), we miss what is most important to them — opportunities to "express and share their gifts, skills, capacities, and abilities."[22] The only way communities can become stronger, he argues, is by harnessing the sum of everyone's capacities.

Communities where public life is vibrant also seem to have a different mind-set about power. So a checkup should look at the way power is defined. Power usually implies control over scarce resources and a legal license to act. This kind of power is assumed to be finite, in limited supply. That is, particular people and institutions are thought to have the power or authority to act, while others are seen — and often see themselves — as

---

20 Grisham, *It Can Be Done,* chap. 2.

21 John P. Kretzmann and John L. McKnight, *Building Communities from the Inside Out: A Path toward Finding and Mobilizing a Community's Assets* (Evanston, Ill.: Center for Urban Affairs and Policy Research, Neighborhood Innovations Network, Northwestern University, 1993).

22 John L. McKnight, "Do No Harm: Policy Options That Meet Human Needs," *Social Policy* 20 (summer 1989): 5–15.

powerless. It follows that those without power can be empowered only by the powerful, and only by the kind of power that comes from control over existing resources.[23]

Where public life is robust, on the other hand, people see that there are many kinds of political power, that even those who have no formal authority have other sources of influence and effect. Some citizen groups are finding that power is an expanding resource, which can be created and re-created. From their perspective, the only true power is the power that people generate themselves; it grows out of their innate capacities and is amplified through their relationships and their ability to band together. It is public power. Power given by others isn't real power. (Educators, take note: while professionals like to talk about empowering people, many citizens aren't pleased to be the objects of someone else's empowerment.)

Seeing power as innate leads to the conviction that "local people must solve local problems," another of Tupelo's guiding principles. In other communities, citizens have said, "We are the solution," echoing an old song from the civil rights movement: "We Are the Ones We Have Been Waiting For." These expressions are affirmations of responsibility, evidence of people "owning" their problems.

Willingness to claim responsibility is essential to generating public power, according to Harry Boyte, who has studied a great many communities and the extent to which they own their problems. Others have come to the same conclusion. In an area of western Connecticut hard hit by plant closings, one citizen explained the need to claim responsibility this way: "All workers have to realize that we're responsible for our own condition. If we don't devote some time to our unions, our political party, our church organization, and the laws being enacted, we'll wake up and

---

23 No one has described this concept better than Harry C. Boyte in works like *Community Is Possible: Repairing America's Roots* (New York: Harper and Row, 1984), *Commonwealth: A Return to Citizen Politics* (New York: Free Press, 1989), "The Growth of Citizen Politics: Stages in Local Community Organizing," *Dissent* 37 (fall 1990): 513–518, and "Beyond Deliberation: Citizenship as Public Work," *Newsletter of PEGS* 5 (spring 1995): 15–19.

find ourselves with empty pension funds, bankrupt companies, disproportionate sacrifices, and a run-down community."[24] A newspaper editor in Wichita expressed the same conviction: "The only way . . . for the community to be a better place to live is for the people of the community to understand and accept their personal responsibility for what happens."[25]

One caveat: a willingness to take responsibility and the conviction that local people have to solve their own problems doesn't mean that communities with a healthy public life are introverted. Not at all. In fact, as learning communities they are constantly trying to find out what others are doing. Tupelo has sent study groups around the country and has brought in scores of outsiders for advice and counsel. But learning communities like Tupelo are adaptive, not imitative. Rather than importing models from elsewhere they create their own.

Taking Stock of the Relationship between Citizens and Institutions

The habit of claiming responsibility seems to affect the way people in communities relate to governments and other major institutions (schools, for instance). Where public life is strong, people are less dependent on institutions like governments, although their governments tend to be relatively effective and well liked. Where public life is weak, on the other hand, people are much more dependent on their governments, which appears to make them unpopular and may contribute to their ineffectiveness.[26]

Schools seem to be subject to a similar "law." In Tupelo, while a great many community organizations educate young people, these other educating institutions in no way detract from the quality or popularity of the public schools. To the contrary, Grisham describes the school system as

---

24 Jeremy Brecher and Tim Costello, eds., *Building Bridges: The Emerging Grassroots Coalition of Labor and Community* (New York: Monthly Review Press, 1990), p. 93.

25 Davis Merritt, Jr., Public Journalism Seminar sponsored by Kettering Foundation and New Directions for News, transcript, December 1992, Kettering Foundation, Dayton, Ohio, p. 9.

26 For more on these tendencies, see Putnam's *Making Democracy Work,* especially pp. 163-181, and Seymour Martin Lipset's "Malaise and Resiliency in America," *Journal of Democracy* 6 (July 1995): 4-18.

"a multifaceted jewel in Tupelo's crown of achievements."[27] Evidence of support is apparent everywhere. A community foundation created to provide private funds for the public schools has received donations larger than the state universities have had in some years. Supporting the public schools is a strong community tradition, though the town is tolerant of those who choose to send their children to private institutions.

Tupelo's citizens are evidently comfortable dealing with their schools. They talk readily and easily about them as part of the community and its public life. There are any number of "doors" into the schools. Businesses, civic groups, churches, and community organizations all have links with them. And citizens expect educators to tap into the community when they are deciding important issues. People also see their schools as one of the ties that bind the community. The schools not only profit from public life, they help maintain it.

Schools are seen quite differently where public life is failing. People talk about them as being detached from the community; they see few links between the schools and other institutions. The dominant concern is "taking care of *my* child" rather than educating *every* child. Instead of uniting citizens, the schools are part of the battleground where a fragmented community fights over narrow interests. In this atmosphere, public schools find it virtually impossible to garner the support they need to be successful.[28]

Looking for the Sources of a Sense of Community and Norms of Cooperation

Visiting Tupelo, researchers have been struck by the powerful sense of community, shared purposes, and norms that direct civic action. While some consider these prerequisites for a healthy public life, my guess is that they are actually the products of public work. In other words, communities don't start out with norms of cooperation; they are created over time, as people work together.

27 Grisham, *It Can Be Done,* chap. 2.
28 The Harwood Group, "Forming Public Capital," p. 4.

My impression that norms grow out of common work is based, in part, on conclusions of the Humphrey Institute, where Harry Boyte has found that citizens have to act together before they can establish a norm that makes cooperation a habit. He reports that, when groups with differing views on affirmative action, gay rights, and abortion have been able to work together, the experience has created stronger public relationships and reduced moral polarization — conditions essential to establishing norms of cooperation.[29] At Kettering we have found (particularly by watching those National Issues Forums held by community organizations) that taking part in any aspect of problem solving — renaming a problem, deliberating with others in making a decision about how to act, carrying out a civic project, judging the results — encourages a sense of community and disposes people to work together in the future.

In addition, the experience of working together often generates stories that create a common memory of how problems are solved. In Tupelo, the story is about people responding to the devastation caused by a tornado. Actually, the storm didn't occur until sometime after the civic and economic revival had begun, which suggests that the account of the town's response to this natural disaster was intentionally selected to convey the norm (working together) that the community wanted to reinforce. Norms like this one prompt people to move beyond their immediate worries and frustrations in order to act with others.

In contrast, a community where public life is weak often embraces destructive norms — people tend to point fingers and blame others, or they say, "We can't [or don't] do that here." These norms limit a community's ability to confront problems head-on. People may be aware that something is wrong yet lack the confidence to change the situation.

Gleaning the norms and feelings of a community from the stories people tell is certainly an important part of a checkup. It may be even more important, however, to look for projects of common work, where constructive habits and a renewed sense of cooperation are generated. No

29 Boyte, "Beyond Deliberation," p. 19.

community's norms are so pervasive that everyone subscribes to them, and not everyone shares even the strongest sense of community solidarity. Healthy communities have always had to reach out to those who are on the outside looking in.

The Challenge

To repeat what I said earlier: for all the lessons they offer, Tupelo and other communities with a healthy public life don't "prove" that public schools will flourish if we strengthen the civil infrastructure of our communities. As I've tried to show, however, there are many reasons to suspect that the well-being of schools is directly related to the state of public life. Certainly Tupelo has recognized this connection. The community seems to have a set of objectives that put a premium on many kinds of education, and the schools seem to draw a broad mandate from these objectives. This doesn't mean that people work at strengthening public life (or "community development," as they call it) simply to have good schools. A healthy public life is something that is valued in and of itself. Those who place a premium on public life value it because they like to live in places where citizens "understand and accept their personal responsibility for what happens."

I am aware that strengthening public life for its own sake may strike harried educators worried about the fate of the next tax levy as a distraction they can ill afford. Local school boards may be so intent on evaluating personnel on the basis of students' test scores that educators don't feel free to spend time on community building. Still, there is no escaping the logic which insists that public schools can't exist without publics.

Our hope, in publishing this book, is that some communities will take up the next challenge, which is to find the way to revitalizing public life where it is weak. Communities are more alike than is popular to say, yet civic invention — which is what distinguishes towns like Tupelo — requires that each of them find its own way. While no one should expect the way to be neat, linear, and systematic, neither does it have to remain mysterious. Communities should start on the journey only after they have mapped the terrain as best they can, sorting out the variables and identifying things that can be changed. They need to keep careful notes of what happens along the way, so that they — and all of us — can learn from their experiments. Above all, they should remember the most important lesson from communities like Tupelo — that their citizens are committed to practicing a different kind of politics, one that brings with it a different way of living together. This kind of politics puts people at the very center of things. It puts a premium on public choice, public deliberation, and public action, not as techniques, but as a way of life.

The Kettering Foundation hopes there are communities trying to rebuild the relationship between the public and the public schools by starting with the public. We'd like to hear about them.

I N D E X